Y2K

A system-wide checklist for your business

About the author

Conor Sexton is an independent systems consultant. He runs his company, Trigraph Software Research, from Dublin in Ireland. He has had six previous books published under the Butterworth-Heinemann, Newnes and Made Simple imprints; these have dealt with the COBOL, C and C++ programming languages, as well as client/server technologies.

Conor has more than 20 years' experience of all aspects of software design, programming, project management and systems implementation. In addition to the programming languages mentioned, he has specialist knowledge of the UNIX, OS/2 and Windows NT operating systems, gained during implementation of a number of development, migration and Y2K-related projects.

Conor Sexton worked for 15 years for a number of multinational software companies before going independent in the early 1990s. Since then, he has consulted, in Ireland, the United Kingdom and more widely in Europe, with IBM, Amdahl Corp., Microsoft WPG, Philips Austria GmbH and CBT Systems Inc. He currently specialises in large-scale systems management and Y2K-related development projects. He has in recent years led, and had extensive hands-on involvement with, a number of major projects in these areas on behalf of major European financial and industrial enterprises. He brings this experience of total project implementation to his latest publication, *Y2K, A system-wide checklist for your business.*

Y2K

A system-wide checklist for your business

CONOR SEXTON

OXFORD AUCKLAND BOSTON JOHANNESBURG MELBOURNE NEW DELHI

Butterworth-Heinemann
Linacre House, Jordan Hill, Oxford OX2 8DP
225 Wildwood Avenue, Woburn, MA 01801-2041
A division of Reed Educational and Professional Publishing Ltd

℞ A member of the Reed Elsevier plc group

First published 1999
© Conor Sexton 1999

TRADEMARKS/REGISTERED TRADEMARKS
Computer hardware and software brand names mentioned in this book are protected
by their respective trademarks and are acknowledged.

British Library Cataloguing in Publication Data
A catalogue record for this book is available from the British Library

ISBN 0 7506 3919 9

🐑 Typeset by P.K.McBride, Southampton
Printed and bound in Great Britain

PLANT A TREE
BTCV
British Trust for
Conservation Volunteers

FOR EVERY TITLE THAT WE PUBLISH, BUTTERWORTH-HEINEMANN
WILL PAY FOR BTCV TO PLANT AND CARE FOR A TREE.

Contents

Preface

This book is intended as an overview for the technical manager of the 'issues' to be considered as part of implementing any Year 2000 (Y2K) repair project. A book such as this must of nature be generic — it cannot refer in particular to your organisation — but it can set out a series of thought-provoking questions which, if answered, will go a long way to addressing your organisation's Y2K problem and its resolution. If this book clarifies the nature of the Y2K problem for you, or if it introduces aspects of the problem that you had not thought of before, then it has succeeded in its purpose.

Most Y2K publications concentrate on repairing software found on the central computers — mainframes or other servers — of large enterprises such as banks, oil companies and governments. This problem and its solution are actually quite well understood, which is probably why those publications concentrate on this area. But server software, although important, is only a minority part of the Y2K problem.

Most large — and small — businesses today maintain a lot of personal computers 'on the periphery': at branch offices, depots and outlying locations. In its most mundane use, the PC has replaced the typewriter and has become indispensable. The PC may additionally be used as a 'client', running enquiry and update software that interacts with an 'engine' program running on a remote server. It is not enough to take the traditional approach, and Y2K-fix just the server software. The client PCs must be made ready also. Because there are so many of them — even in small businesses — this is where the less-well-known Y2K problem is found. Even if your organisation is small — you are not running a large bank and you do not own a mainframe — the fact that you use PCs to keep it running means that the Y2K problem affects you, too. Use this book as a checklist of the Y2K issues you should at least be thinking about.

This book is deliberately short. A number of its competitors — mostly from the US — are in my view, both over-hyped and over-padded. In seven chapters, I cover the essence of the Y2K problem and measures that should be adopted to fix it. In giving emphasis to the distributed client/server computing model, as well as the traditional mainframe home of the Y2K problem, the concerns of small business as well as major enterprises are addressed. In fact, the approach taken here to the solution of Y2K is driven by the component nature of the client/server architecture.

Chapter 1 states the Year 2000 problem in short and without hype. It also, for fun and enlightenment, gives a summary of the 6,000-year history of our calendar and where the Y2K difficulty came from in the first place. Chapter 2 covers the manifestations of Y2K: its effects on computer systems and business, but without the 'defuse-the-timebomb' hyperbole beloved of so many publications on the subject. Chapter 3 outlines the essential components of any project plan directed at effecting the Y2K repair in a large or small business.

Chapter 4 takes a model of the client/server architecture and uses it, component by component, to identify where the Y2K fixes are necessary and what they are. This part should be of interest to small businesses that do not have the large server and software base characteristic of larger organisations, but for whom the problem resides in their stock of client PCs. Chapter 5 addresses the traditional programming aspects of Y2K, with actual code solutions shown in complete COBOL programs. If programming is not your 'thing', you can, without much loss, skip the COBOL and read the English only. For those prepared to examine the code, the solutions presented should prove instructive. Chapter 6 deals with testing the Y2K repairs once they are applied. Chapter 7 presents a collection of software utilities, useful Y2K Web sites, with a UK bias, and some closing recommendations on how to conduct your repair effort.

In addressing Year 2000, this book consciously leans towards the kind of distributed client/server computing environment, heavily reliant on PCs, found in most large and small businesses today. I hope you find it useful.

Conor Sexton, 1999

1 The Y2K problem

1.1 Summary description

The acronym Y2K can be regarded as a microcosm of the Year 2000 problem itself – a case of abbreviated data. The essence of the Year 2000 difficulty is that, to save space and processing on legacy (pre-1996) systems, years were represented as two digits — say, 75 for 1975 – on the assumption that the code or firmware doing year processing would be replaced before the year 2000. Because of the sheer scale of investment in the commercial software and hardware of these systems, this has not happened. The danger now is that the year '00' will be regarded by existing programs, operating systems and hardware as 1900, not 2000. An associated problem is that 2000 is a leap year, while 1900 was not. This completes the statement of the Y2K problem.

The effects of the Y2K problem are myriad. The purpose of this book is to describe its consequences, and the management and technical actions needed to forestall and overcome the problem, particularly in the small-to-medium-sized business environment. What this book tries to avoid are the frenzied and overlong 'what-if' /'shock-horror' depictions of the consequences given in many existing publications on the subject.

In general, because of Y2K, any computer system that does any date processing – aged debt reporting; calculation of the system date – is likely to do its processing wrongly on, or even before, the arrival of the Year 2000.

The Y2K problem is a simple one. The fix is almost equally simple. The difficulty is that dates are everywhere in almost all computer systems, so the simple fix must be done in millions of places.

At least as regards fixing application software, there are two broad lines of attack:

- Expand the date-representation used in software from YYMMDD to CCYYMMDD (where CC is the century), expand file and other data accordingly, and alter program logic where necessary.

- Instead of expanding the date, use a 'window' scheme in which the century runs from, say 1961 to 2060. The two-digit 75 is then taken to mean 1975, while 25 becomes 2025. Program logic must be altered.

The Y2K problem came about in the days of centralised legacy (usually mainframe) computer systems. It mostly shows itself in programs written during the 1960s, 1970s and 1980s in the COBOL business language, although software expressed in languages such as Fortran, PL/1, RPG, C and C++, is affected as well.

The computing world has moved on since the mainframe-only era. Distributed client/server systems have been widely adopted; the client side of the relationship is most commonly in the form of the PC workstation, with the server part being a larger computer system connected to the client by network and running the 'number crunching' part of the distributed application. An example is an airline-reservation system. The travel agent enters an enquiry or reservation to a 'front-end' application program running on a client workstation. This is refined and transmitted over the network to the server for processing by the 'engine' at the 'back end'. The server returns the response to the client for display. Although they are newer than centralised computer systems, this does not stop client/server architectures from hosting the Y2K problem. In the client/server context, therefore, the problem must be considered from the perspectives of client, network, server and data exchange.

Benefits of fixing the Y2K problem

Fixing the Y2K problems in your organisation's computer hardware and software – and in data files imported and exported – can have beneficial direct effects and side-effects including these:

- Systems will continue to work in the period before, during and after the 1999–2000 roll-over.

- There may be business gains at the expense of organisations that have not prepared as well as yours.

- If your organisation can demonstrate commitment to fixing the problem, any litigation charges will be ameliorated.

- In assessing your systems as part of the Y2K project effort, you should gain new knowledge of your base of hardware and software.

- Some software will likely be eliminated, streamlining your organisation's software base.

- Other changes – most commonly upgrading clients to a new operating system such as Windows NT – can be implemented 'on the back of' the Y2K effort, thereby (in theory, at least) reducing the cost of killing multiple birds with one stone.

The calendar

The Y2K problem has come about because of quirks in the Western calendar. Understanding the origin of these quirks is not necessary to solving the Y2K problem but is useful and, to some people, interesting. The following several pages are the only somewhat whimsical part of this book; skip them if you want to skip the history.

1.2 Genesis: a short history of our calendar

The Y2K dependency is caused by using two digits to represent a four-digit quantity such as the year 1975. The representation 19990128 for January 28, 1999 refers to the *Gregorian calendar*, after the 16th century Pope Gregory XIII. Gregory's calendar is rooted in the fact that (currently) it takes the Earth 365 days, 5 hours, 48 minutes and 46 seconds to orbit the Sun, that period of time being the *solar year*.

Calendric origins

In the first efforts to codify the passage of time in the form of a calendar, humanity got it wrong. The ancient Greeks, Chinese and Sumerians, among others, relied on the lunar year – a succession of twelve lunar periods of about 29½ days each. This resulted in a year of close to 354 days. This mapping of the real solar year ran about 11 days too fast. Over several years, the calendar would fall out of step with the seasons and the solstices, the latter actually interchanging, according to the calendar, in a period of between 16 and 17 years.

The lunar year proved unworkable, particularly for farmers who had real seasons to deal with. In a first effort at improvement, the Babylonians instituted a 360-day year, with each day of 24 hours. The reasons for their using 360 are unknown, although the number became the basis of our modern compass. The number 24 was based on the twelve signs of the Zodiac, with both night and day being expressed in terms of the twelve signs.

The ancient Egyptians were the first to use a solar year and were also the first to measure approximately the length of that year. Around 4000 BC, based on yearly-occurring high-water flood marks on the Nile, they calculated the year to be about 365 days long. Astronomical observations of the yearly conjunction of the rising Sun and the star Sirius allowed the Egyptians to refine that measurement to a remarkably accurate 365¼ days. This is, in essence, the year we use today.

The Julian calendar

Until the time of Julius Caesar, the Roman calendar had been lunar, like that of the Greeks. The first Roman calendar, propagated by Romulus in 753 BC, was of 304 days organised in ten months. Under this calendar, the year started in Martis (named after the god of War); continued through Aprilis, Maius and Junius (named after other Roman gods); and finished, unimaginatively, with Quintilis,

Sextilis, Septembris, Octobris, Novembris and Decembris. So it is that the 9th, 10th, 11th and 12th months of our calendar were originally the 7th, 8th, 9th and 10th months of the Romulan calendar.

The 304-day calendar was even less practical in use than the 354 lunar measurement. The early Romans quickly changed the number of days to 354. Over the next several centuries, ad-hoc additions of days were made to line up the calendar with the observed seasons and solstices. Confusion still abounded, with trade being disrupted and unscrupulous legislators taking advantage of the imprecise calendar to lengthen their terms of office. In 46 BC, at the height of his world power, Julius Caesar decided to sort out the calendar once and for all.

Caesar, on the advice of his Alexandrian court astronomer Sosigenes, adopted on behalf of Imperial Rome, the best approximation to the length of the solar year yet made, 365¼ days. He also moved the start of the year from March to January 1st – a change not taken up until much later in various parts of the world. Caesar also inaugurated the system of leap years that is the essence of what we know today: every fourth year carried an extra day to take account of the fraction in 365¼.

To bring the year to 365 days, Caesar specified that every month except February should be of length alternating between 30 and 31 days. March was of 31 days, April 30, May 31, June 30, July 31, August 30, and so on. February was 29 days in an ordinary year and 30 in a leap year.

These changes were adopted by acclamation and used throughout the Roman world. In recognition of Caesar's achievement, the Roman Senate renamed the month of Quintilis to become Julius (July).

Around the time of Christ, the Emperor Augustus made further (unnecessary) changes to Caesar's calendar. In his own honour, he changed the name of Sextilis to Augustus. Then, not wanting that month to be one day shorter than Julius, he increased its length from 30 to 31. He then changed the lengths of the next four months from 31, 30, 31 and 30 respectively to the lengths we know today. Thus, September is of 30 days, October 31, November 30 and December 31. To compensate for the extra day in August, the Emperor reduced the number of days in February to 28 in an ordinary year and 29 in a leap year.

Emperor Constantine

We now move forward almost 400 years, into the era of a declining, Christianised, Roman Empire. In an effort to standardise the date of Easter – and resolve other ecclesiastical disputes – Constantine convened in 325 AD, the Council of Nicaea. In the event, the Council standardised several changes:

- The seven-day week

- Sunday as the first, holy, day of the week

- Fixing of Christian feast dates, including Christmas

- An agreed placement of Easter day.

The seven days were decided on as one for each of the then-known 'planets' in the solar system, including the Sun and Moon but excluding the Earth. This gives us the names Sunday and Monday; a knowledge of the French language shows that Mardi (Tuesday) represents Mars, Mercredi (Wednesday) stands for Mercury, Jeudi (Thursday) is Jupiter and Vendredi (Friday) represents Venus. Saturday, even in English, is for the planet Saturn. The English midweek day-names are Anglo-Saxon corruptions that arose centuries later. For example, Jupiter's day (Thursday) is so named in English after the Saxon god of fire, Thor.

The adopted Easter date was based both in the Julian solar calendar and in the Jewish lunar calendar in use at the time of Christ. Because the resurrection of Christ had been recorded on a Sunday, Easter was fixed as the first Sunday following the first full moon after the spring equinox.

With these matters settled, and with the incipient descent of Europe into the obscurantist Dark Ages, further enquiry into and development of the calendar was confined mainly into methods of determining the day on which Easter actually fell, based on the Nicaean rules.

The Gregorian calendar

Even with the accuracy and convenience of the Julian Calendar, the actual year is 11 minutes and 14 seconds shorter than 365¼ days. Over a long period of years, the 'drift' began to show when relating the calendar date to the Sun's position. In the mid-1570s, Pope Gregory XIII set up a calendric commission to solve this problem and to fix dates in the Catholic ecclesiastic calendar, particularly reforms instituted by the Council of Trent (1545–63).

Two members of the commission were the Italian doctor Aloysius Lilius and the Jesuit astronomer Christopher Clavius. The latter was responsible mainly for piloting through the Church political system the elegant system of changes proposed by Lilius.

The calendar commission presented its proposals to Gregory in 1581. The length of the solar year was established at 365 days, 5 hours, 49 minutes and 12 seconds, this being an average of various measurements previously taken of the Sun's (apparent!) orbit around the earth and of the intervals between solstices. This measurement is about 26 seconds slower than the solar year as measured now. This average day-length runs a little less than eleven minutes short of the ¼ day in the Julian year. This 'drift' approximates closely to one day every 134 years, or three days every 400 years.

Lilius adjusted by means of an added refinement. Henceforth, century-years – including 1700, 1800 and 1900 – would not be leap years but century-years divisible evenly by 400 would. This reduced the 'drift' inaccuracy to around 26 seconds a year. We consider this acceptable and we still use the Gregorian system. It also means that 2000 is a leap year while that other '00' year, 1900, is not.

Among the critics of Lilius' system was one Joseph Scaliger. Scaliger nevertheless used the Gregorian calendar as a basis for calculation of his day-calendar system, which traced history using days only and completely independently of years measured as being of a mean length. Derived from Scaliger's calculations is the confusingly-named Julian date (first form, and distinct from the Julian calendar referred to above), so named because Scaliger's father's name was Julius. This counts the days from midday on 1 January 4713 BC.

Adoption of the Gregorian calendar

The calendar commission's changes were implemented throughout Catholic Europe starting in 1582. Gregory instituted a one-time 'catch-up' for the 1600 years of 'drift' that had preceded his changes. He eliminated the dates 5 October 1582 to 14 October 1582 (inclusive of both) to compensate. October was selected because it had few religious feasts that would be lost by the elimination of ten days. By 1588 the complying Catholic countries of Europe, from Portugal to Hungary, had fallen into line with the Vatican.

Protestant England and Germany resisted. England's Queen Elizabeth I was receptive to the change – although proposed by a Pope – to the extent that the science behind it was good. The Archbishop of Canterbury, however, blocked the reform. The attempted Spanish invasion of England in 1588 ensured that England would remain on 'Old Style' time, out of step with its European neighbours, for another 170 years.

The various states of Germany adopted the Gregorian calendar in the early 1700s, with England (now part of Britain, after the 1707 Act of Union) following suit in 1752. By this time, one more day needed to be deleted to get rid of the 'drift'. So the eleven days 3 September to 13 September 1752 (inclusive of both) disappeared from the calendar. Because of the pre-eminence of British power in the 18th and 19th centuries, the British system was adopted and these dates disappeared from the Gregorian calendar used by the Western world.

An interesting side-effect of the British change was its contemporaneous adoption of 1 January as New Year's Day. This done, the old New Year tax collection date of 25 March was not changed. The dropped 11 days rendered this 5 April by the new calendar. The latter date has remained the end of the tax year in Britain and Ireland ever since.

Many countries adopted the Gregorian calendar in the 1800s, notably Japan in 1873. Countries of the Eastern Orthodox Church followed in the early 20th century, with China nearly completing the worldwide spread of the Calendar in 1949.

Other dates

Because Gregory and Caesar failed to assign a year zero, centuries run from 1 through 100. Therefore, of course, the 21st century begins in the year 2001 and not 2000.

A side-effect of the Gregorian calendar is the establishment of the Lilian date (after Lilius): in this system, dates are represented by counting from 14 October 1582, which is treated as day zero. Surprisingly, this form is often used commercially, especially by IBM.

There is an ANSI/ISO date also, counting the days from 31 December 1600, which is treated as day zero.

There is yet another Julian date (second form, and also distinct from the Julian calendar!), which is very widely used in commercial software. With this, the date is represented either as a five-digit or as a seven-digit quantity: 28 January 1999 is stored either as 99028 or as 1999028. When searching for Y2K dependencies, this must be watched for as well as dates of the YYMMDD form; Julian dates (second form) are everywhere.

Finally, to be characteristically different, the UNIX operating system calculates all its times in seconds from the start of January 1, 1970. It uses a long integer (32 bits) to do so and, as such, can increment from zero up to 2,147,483,647 seconds. There are 31,556,926 seconds in a solar year (refer to 365 days, 5 hours...). Thus, the UNIX timing scheme is good for slightly over 68 years – which means we run into the wall early in 2038. Therein lies another Year 2000-like dependency, unless before 2038 they implement the number of seconds in 64 bits.

To the 21st century

The remainder of this book concentrates on how to manage computer systems of all kinds such that they correctly handle a number of aspects of the date conventions explained above. 2000 is a leap year but 1900 and 2100 are not. 95 must not be assumed to be 1995. The Julian (second form) date 74058 must not automatically be assumed to be 27 February 1974. File and display screen designs must provide space for the whole year-identifier – 1944 or 2044 – to be stored.

The problem is a simple one and has been shamelessly over-hyped. Its manifestations (and solutions) are many-faceted, and it is these we consider next.

2 | Implications of Y2K for your business

2.1 General manifestation of Y2K

As I point out in Chapter 1, Y2K potentially affects all parts of the conventional client/server system: the client (usually PCs); the network, in particular routers and bridges; and the back-end mainframe, minicomputer, UNIX or Windows NT/2000 server. Y2K is not confined to mainframes and COBOL programs, although that is where the problem is found in its most concentrated form. In fact, it can be more difficult to fix client problems arising from Y2K than those occurring on a server. A server is by definition at least to a degree centralised, which reduces the travel and deployment aspect of fixing it. But how do you arrange to run a BIOS-checking program on 1,000 or 10,000 widely-distributed PCs? How do you then deploy the fix to the PCs that need it? There is more on this subject in Chapter 4. BIOS, incidentally, is the PC's Basic Input/ Output System; it maintains in software the date as stored in the CMOS (Complementary Metal-Oxide Semiconductor!) memory area.

Y2K manifests itself on PCs mainly with a wrong system date. Older and other non-Y2K-compliant PCs either fail to handle a four-digit year beginning with '2' or fail to 'remember' such a date between power-down and power-up.

The Y2K problem may cause computer networks to malfunction. This is most likely on wide-area networks (WANs) containing nodes distributed across more than one timezone. At some point in the 48 hours between 0001 on December 31, 1999 and 2400 on January 1, 2000, two distributed systems in different timezones will record different dates. Whether or not the infrastructure stays operational is then a function of the network operating system, hubs, routers and network application software.

On the server side, or in a centralised mainframe system, Y2K affects commercial applications in the main. These are mostly written in COBOL. The minority is those date-dependent programs written in RPG, PL/1, Fortran and even the more modern C and C++. Typical date-dependent commercial applications include mortgage, insurance, pension, tax, financial, stock-control, personnel, age-calculation and futures – in short, almost the whole gamut of business software as it is currently known. Possible effects of date-dependencies include:

- Renewal notices: the computer fails to send a notice that your insurance is going to expire on a date after January 1, 2000.

- Invoices and invoice reminders might not be sent if the dates straddle 1999 and 2000; cash flow will be hurt as a result.

- There may be a consequent rush of catch-up invoice generation – the system thinks you have not been sent any invoices or insurance renewals for many years!

- A payments-tracking system might decide in January 2000 that all customers invoiced in December 1999 were seriously in arrears, possibly starting debt-collection measures.

- In stock systems, just-in-time deliveries to the production line may fail if the dispatching program gets its dates wrong.

- Credit-card or licensing systems might fail to handle '00' (or later) expiry dates, judging such dates to have already expired and invalidating the card or licence.

- Reports sequenced on year may be wrong: 2000 will *precede* 1999 and 1975.

- Day-of-week calculations predicated on a 00–99 year range will be wrong.

- Calculations involving intervals – particularly periodic interest-calculation – may be in error where the period straddles 1999 and 2000.

- If '00' or '99' are used as error-indicators in date calculations, a program will fail. In the case of '99', the problem is brought forward by a year.

- If '00' or '99' are used as end-of-file markers, programs testing these markers may fail either in 1999 or 2000.

- 9 September 1999. Watch for this one; there is a long-standing habit among COBOL programmers of using 'all-nines' to represent an impossible or error condition. If your organisation's programs start failing on that Thursday morning, think of this.

- The system date may be generated wrongly. For example, the DATE built-in function in the COBOL language returns a two-digit year. The fact that this is an aspect of a language standardised as recently as 1985 is strange but true.

Very few programs on either client or server systems are unaffected, at least potentially, by the Y2K problem. Examples of programs most likely not to be affected include games and simple text processing modules. The bulk of commercial software, however, makes heavy use of dates. This is particularly true of programs that manipulate money.

Most money has no tangible existence. It is present only as a number stored on a computer. If there is a large number stored in the name of your organisation, then you have 'money' in your account. If a Y2K-related bug in bank software handling the account wrongly withdraws money multiple times, fails to add interest, subtracts too much interest, or removes your credit rating, your organisation may end up with the number zero to its name. Then you really have no money.

All the above are considerations affecting commercial software. Less familiar are such aspects as hard-coded dates in computers, VCRs, cars and, in essence, any device that can be programmed with a date and time. Less familiar also, and more frightening, are security and defence applications: what will happen, on January 1, 2000, to the world's nuclear power stations and ballistic missiles? With luck, at worst, they will 'fail-safe' and just shut down.

2.2 Budget and cost

Faced with a problem like Y2K, it is possible to adopt the 'ostrich approach' and do nothing, hoping that any problems arising can be solved on an ad-hoc basis. The cost of this approach cannot be quantified because, without investigation, we have no way of knowing how well our software will operate when 2000 arrives or how successfully it will interact with third-party software and data.

Most organisations have chosen not to ignore Y2K and are devoting significant resources to investigating and solving the problem as it affects them. Neither this nor any other book can quantify the cost of this effort for *your* particular organisation. What it can do is give some rules of thumb about the likely cost and set out the areas in which costs are likely to be incurred.

One rule of thumb is to multiply the number of lines of code to be fixed by a money amount such as UK£1.00 or US$1.50, giving the approximate overall cost of the Y2K repair effort. In a typical mainframe-based commercial installation, there might be 100 COBOL applications or modules averaging 3,000 lines each. We derive £300,000 as the assumed cost of the Y2K project.

One problem with this measure is that, as 2000 approaches and resources for fixing the Y2K problem become more scarce, the cost per line of code is increasing. The numbers I have quoted may be too low. A more serious difficulty is that the measure is too restrictive: it is biased toward the centralised mainframe-based computing model where all the application software has been developed in-house and where the source-code of that software is under our control. The most obvious Y2K-related cost is indeed that of fixing centralised (often COBOL) software written by our own software developers between the 1960s and 1980s. But there are a myriad of other costs which are less obvious but may total more.

Listed below are typical costs associated with a Y2K repair project. I have presented these in summary form grouped for clarity under six headings:

- Hardware
- Software
- Configuration management
- Staff
- Business
- Legal

Many books and publications present extensive 'what-if' scenarios with these headings along the lines of: 'if data sent to a supplier is not Y2K-clean, then your just-in-time stock management system will fail, with catastrophic results for the business...'. Such scenarios tend to result in rather long books and publications but are usually of little practical use to your operation. It is more useful to present here a fairly comprehensive summary of potential cost items as a checklist that you should consider. You are then the one best placed to decide how they apply (or not) to your organisation. The list follows.

Hardware

- In a centralised or client/server system, one or more test servers will be required to test Y2K-repaired applications before putting them into production.

- Y2K-repaired software may be slightly slower than the original – because of expanded data and date-windowing logic. Although the speed decrease will not be critical, it may influence a decision to change the production server anyway.

- Extra servers may be rented or leased, which is 'dead money' spent. It is probably more useful to keep them as test and development systems post-Year 2000.

- More disk space will be required to handle data files with expanded dates. There will also be a temporary space requirement to accommodate testing, as well as storage of multiple versions of applications during migration to production.

- Particularly in client/server implementations, there will be a large requirement for new PCs. Obsolete PCs, and ones with BIOS systems unable to accommodate a century switch, will be replaced.

- Many systems managers take the opportunity presented by the Y2K repair effort to upgrade PC operating systems. It is common practice right now to replace Windows 3.x and OS/2 environments with Windows NT/2000 as part of the Y2K project. The cost of licence fees must be taken into account here, as well as the considerable cost of large-scale migration of desktop operating systems.

- In some cases, it may be possible to reprogram BIOS systems to handle multiple centuries, or to replace obsolete BIOS chips. The costs here are those of BIOS software and new BIOS chips. There may be hidden compatibility costs: can you be sure that your PCs will work with new BIOSs or that the original PC suppliers will continue to support them after the change?

Software

- Home-grown application software for mainframes and servers must be checked for Y2K dependencies and, if necessary, modified. The cost of this part of the Y2K effort, at least, is calculable in terms of cost per line of code.

- Y2K software tools will be required to check such code for dependencies. There are free utilities that do this, available mainly on the Web, but the good ones are sold by reputable suppliers for a licence fee.

- Application software developed for your organisation by someone else will also have to be checked and fixed. If the original supplier is still around they may fix it – for a price.

- In the case of client/server applications developed in-house, the client part – usually the presentation/enquiry 'front-end' – must be checked in the same way as the 'back-end' application code on the server.

- PC-based shrink-wrapped application software, and older operating systems, must be made Y2K-compliant. In some cases, free upgrades may be available; mostly there will be an upgrade fee per desktop.

- Extra training will be required for users of upgraded PC applications and operating systems.

Configuration management

- A central part of the Y2K project is getting an inventory of the systems and software that constitute your computing environment. This is not easy, particularly in large distributed client/server implementations. Software tools – at a cost – are usually required for the job.

- Existing home-grown application software must be sized in terms of lines of code. Any software that can simply be scrapped must be identified.

- Software tools for checking client PCs must be deployed to and loaded on those PCs. If your organisation has 500 or 5,000 client PCs, how physically do you run a BIOS-checking program on them all? The options are either (the most common!) that a technician visits every PC, or that the BIOS software is remotely installed and run on each PC. Either way, there is a cost.

- Similar costs apply to deploying upgraded application or operating system software to a large number of PCs. OS migration in particular is tricky and expensive (see Chapter 4).

Staff

- Project managers, Y2K consultants and other contract Y2K staff may be required. A good Y2K consultant, in identifying pitfalls, can repay the investment but hiring any of these people on a contract basis is expensive and getting more so. In the UK, mainframe COBOL programmers can now command from £300 per day upwards – that is at least £60,000 per year. Y2K consultants and project managers are yet more expensive.

- Attracted by this kind of money, some of your organisation's software staff may leave, adding to your resourcing problems.

- An influx of highly-paid Y2K contract people may cause friction with existing 'permanent' staff. This may affect the progress of the Y2K project, not to speak of causing the departure of 'permanent' people.

Business

- Part of the Y2K repair effort lies in ensuring that data incoming from suppliers and other businesses for use on your systems is Y2K-clean. Data transmitted by your organisation to others must also be 'clean'. Consequences of failure here include the necessity of changing suppliers, and of holding more stock to cover failures. Both activities have an associated cost.

- Even with the best Y2K repair effort, it is likely that some labour-intensive 'fixing' will have to be done early in 2000 in cases where invoices are wrongly generated, reports are not ordered properly, and so on.

- Perhaps the largest business expense is that incurred during parallel running of old and new systems and the disruption caused by migration to the new system. Quantifying this cost is very difficult, measured as it usually is in business delays as well as staff uncertainty and overtime.

Legal

- Cost of litigation, if it is necessary.

- Cost of insurance, if it is available, against Y2K-related liability.

Beneficial Y2K side-effects

All of the above are cost items; most are unavoidable aspects of dealing comprehensively with the Y2K problem. On the positive side, implementing a good Y2K repair project has some cost-saving side-effects. These include:

- 'Killing two birds with one stone': by migrating from a non-Y2K-compliant client operating environment such as Windows 3.11 to, say, Windows NT/2000, you get the OS upgrade as part of the Y2K repair. This is now widespread practice in large organisations.

- Discarding obsolete code: the thorough code analysis required in a Y2K repair project may, as a side-effect, identify software that is unused or which can be otherwise abandoned. It is deeply ingrained with most software developers never irrevocably to delete *anything*; however unnecessary a module appears, they keep it 'just in case'. As the software base accordingly grows, its contents become increasingly obscure and the incentive for anyone to audit it decreases. Y2K forces this audit and may allow rationalisation.

- As a result of the Y2K effort, remaining code may be better documented. This reduces the cost of future maintenance.

- Acquisition of Y2K test servers and expansion of production servers are investments for the future, not just measures forced by the Y2K repair. The cost of these investments can be written off over a period of years and not just assigned to the Y2K budget.

2.3 Legal

There are obviously legal implications of failures of hardware and software caused – or alleged to be caused – by Y2K. For most organisations, the legal issues arise in dealing with suppliers and clients. For example, if, ten years ago, you acquired mainframe-based stock-control software from a third-party supplier that is found now not to be Y2K-compliant, what obligation is on the supplier to fix it? If you bought a PC in 1994 that has a non-Y2K BIOS, can you go now to the supplier demanding an upgrade? In any case, is either supplier still in business?

It is likely that many such Y2K-related legal questions are not explicitly covered by the law of the land and will be more generally dealt with by non-specific legislation such as the UK laws of contract and tort (negligence).

A legal contract exists if there have been offer, acceptance and consideration: a supplier offered to sell me something; I accepted the offer and paid for the goods or services delivered. A contract does not have to be *written* to be a contract. So, even in absence of contract documents, you still have the possibility of remedy through the courts if you believe that a supplier has not delivered the agreed goods or services. Of course, if there is a written contract containing terms that support your claim, your position in law is rather stronger.

In the case of the 1994 PC, Y2K was probably not even considered part of the terms of sale; you are in a weak position here in trying to have the supplier upgrade, free of charge, the BIOS to be Y2K-compliant. The same is true of the stock-control software supplied in the 1980s. Things might be different, though, with software and hardware more recently acquired. If the stock-control software were supplied in 1997, not 1987, the terms of the contract (written or not) for its supply probably specify Y2K compliance. In this case, there is an obligation on the supplier to ensure that the software is indeed compliant. If it is not and the supplier refuses to fix it, you may successfully sue for the cost of making the fix and for any lost business and profits incurred as a consequence.

Under the UK laws of tort, a supplier may be sued for negligence. For example, stock-control software written in 1997 should be Y2K compliant. If it is not, it is reasonable to assert that it is not *fit for the purpose* for which it is intended. The supplier could as a consequence be held not to have demonstrated *adequate due care and attention* to ensuring that the software will be viable only a few years hence. These factors may form the basis of a negligence claim against the supplier.

Under UK law, where a claim for negligence is triggered by a *latent cause* – a failure, like Y2K, waiting to happen – the negligence claim can only be made within three years of discovery of the cause or when *it should have been discovered*. So, although you may not have been very concerned about Y2K in 1994, you knew – if you thought about it – that it might six years hence affect software purchased then. Your case is accordingly weakened, probably fatally.

From the perspective of your organisation in dealing with clients (that is, where you are the supplier), you can to a great extent defend against the 'due care and attention' eventuality. You should not only ensure that any hardware, software or data you supply are Y2K-compliant but (and perhaps more importantly) you should take care to *document* your Y2K effort and your intention to comply.

In computing, as in many walks of life, 'going to law' is to be avoided if at all possible. There is no such thing as a watertight contract through which a 'coach and horses' cannot be driven. It is best to take the line of having the best possible relations with suppliers and clients, while taking reasonable precautions to avoid both bad acquisitions from suppliers and legal claims by clients. Here is a summary checklist of more legal considerations:

- Retain a legal adviser as a member of your organisation's Y2K project team for the duration of its existence.

- If your organisation exchanges data with a client, get a written statement of their Y2K-compliance requirements – including file and data formats – as part of the process of demonstrating 'effort and intent'.

- Similarly, where data is exchanged with a supplier, send them a statement of your organisation's compliance requirements.

- With both suppliers and clients, assess their readiness for Y2K compliance. You have to allow for the possibility of replacing one or more suppliers if they are simply unwilling to make the necessary Y2K preparations.

- Where contracting for supply of software from a third-party supplier, explicitly specify Y2K-compliance as a requirement.

- Before doing Y2K repair work on third-party-supplied software, assess with the legal adviser the possibility of having the original supplier fix it instead.

- If you do not have the source code for third-party software, the supplier is unlikely to be under an obligation to furnish it. Try to get the source from the supplier on a goodwill basis, rather than going to law on the matter.

- If your organisation does have the source code and intends to carry out the Y2K repair itself, first check your legal entitlement to do so.

- Before repairing third-party software, assess the obligation (and ability) of the supplier to support it after the change has been applied.

- Before doing Y2K repair work on any software, check the (slim) possibility that your organisation may be covered by insurance against the cost.

- Note that the Y2K 'bug' (so-called) is *not* a virus: a virus is, by its very character, malevolent. Y2K is hardly benevolent but the creators of the problem had no malicious intent.

- If your organisation has shareholders, find out which software in your suite affects them most (calculation/notification of dividend payments?) and have the legal adviser assess the risk of the organisation's being sued by one or more shareholders.

- Unlikely, but if your organisation is about to do a company acquisition or merger, first check how much of a Y2K problem is waiting to be inherited.

- Do not write any letters or emails that in any way decry or admit shortcomings in your organisation's Y2K repair effort.

Involvement in legal action may be forced on your organisation, but it is always a monumental waste of time. It is vastly preferable to concentrate on maintaining good relations with clients and suppliers and on working with them to agree the Y2K compliance requirements referred to in the list above.

2.4 Staffing

Four questions dominate consideration of how to staff a Y2K project:
- Who should be involved from a business perspective
- Who should be on the Y2K project team
- How to attract and retain the right people
- Whether or not to use outside suppliers and subcontractors.

Each of these questions is briefly expanded on next.

Business involvement

The most important non-technical group that should be involved in the Y2K project is your own organisation's senior management. As a technical problem considered at the 'micro' level, Y2K is simple. At a business – or 'macro' – level, it is much more difficult. It affects every part of the organisation's IT infrastructure, the interaction of that infrastructure with the IT systems of clients and suppliers, and the day-to-day running of non-IT business. To address appropriately a challenge so pervasive, senior management must be committed to, drive, and approve funding for the Y2K project.

Your organisation does not operate in isolation; it does business with outsiders. If the business partners have different expectations about the data they exchange – we want date-expanded Y2K-compliant formats but a supplier gives us files with 6-digit dates – software on either side will produce meaningless results. To avoid the business repercussions of such failure, the Y2K project must involve IT representatives of clients and suppliers. The most important objective of this liaison is defining the interfaces: all data exchanged must meet an agreed Y2K-compliant format defined as part of the Y2K project and codified in statements of Y2K compliance requirements exchanged between the parties.

As I have noted, legal resources and advice should be available to the Y2K project from its inception.

Non-IT employees of your organisation will have to use the software changed to be Y2K-compliant. Screen and data formats may change. New versions of third-party software will be installed. These employees need training in new procedures and usage, and must be aware of the schedule for migration to systems modified for Y2K compliance.

Y2K project team

The project team should have enough senior management support to ensure 'buy-in' on the part of all users of software and hardware affected by the Y2K problem. The problem must be addressed not just in the context of individual business units within the organisation, but in terms of the interdependence of these units and, in turn, their need to interoperate with outside clients and suppliers.

To manage such dependencies, it is best to establish a centralised Y2K Office, with responsibilities and authority across departments and business units. The Y2K project manager should be a senior manager with technical and business awareness rather than someone who is primarily a technician. The manager's skills should be primarily those of leadership; ability to co-ordinate across departments and organisations; and the project management skills of identifying, scheduling and ensuring the implementation of a myriad of Y2K-related tasks. The project manager should also have 'sign-off authority' to authorise spending within the agreed Y2K budget and the hiring of people.

Apart from the legal representative previously mentioned, the other members of the project team will be primarily technical. To identify who they are, consider the nature of your organisation's IT infrastructure. In the client/server model, we have one or more servers, a network and a lot of client PCs on the periphery. In a mainframe environment, the prevalence of PCs is less, but there is still a network and the mainframe itself runs application software in a manner similar to that of server systems in a client/server network.

The required technical representatives in the project team are at least these:

• The PC specialist. Every organisation has a few; they are the people who know about testing BIOSs, installing video drivers, partitioning disks, and administering PC operating systems.

• The network administrator: the person responsible for ensuring that the traffic load on the network is balanced; maintaining hubs and routers; and making sure that enough network addresses are available to accommodate the users who must be connected.

• The system administrator – 'sysprog' in the mainframe world – the person who manages server systems and keeps them running; ensures that software runs properly and to the required schedule; implements a backup schedule; and deletes unwanted files and data from disk.

• Application programmers to do the Y2K repair work on in-house-developed software. On mainframes, all the software is centralised. In a client/server environment, such applications will have a PC-based 'front-end' as well as the server-resident 'back end' or 'engine'. The team must have programmers for each language in use at the installation. COBOL is in the majority but Assembler, PL/1, Fortran, RPG and even C/C++ expertise may be needed. Front-end client applications may be written with modern tools such as Visual Basic or PowerBuilder, which must also be checked notwithstanding their modernity.

- Testers, both on the client and server sides, to verify the operation of the Y2K-cleaned-up systems.

- Lastly, but not necessarily, one or more Y2K consultants to advise on technical direction, potential problems, software tools, and to give the benefit of experience gained from previous projects.

With the project team in place, it must have the authority to work across departments and business units, to verify any new software as Y2K-compliant before it is acquired by any department, and to monitor the progress of departments in keeping up with the Y2K implementation schedule.

Getting and keeping the right people

Most organisations already have technical staff in the categories listed above. The Y2K staffing difficulty usually arises where the bottleneck is found. This is in the application programming area. PC specialists and network and system administrators are important, but the problem of scalability arises when the server application programs written for or by the organisation over decades must be assessed, examined and fixed. If there are 100 COBOL programs of 3,000 lines each, that is 300,000 lines of code to be checked and possibly modified. The job is complicated if, say, there is a mixture of COBOL and RPG, or if some of the code is written in Assembler. And most corporate software suites are larger than 100 programs.

If more application programmers are needed, there are three possible sources of supply:

- Hire more programmers as regular employees

- Hire programmers on a contract basis

- Induce older programmers, perhaps retired employees of your organisation, to return.

All these options, certainly the first two, are expensive and becoming more so as demand increases. In hiring programmers on a 'permanent' basis, there must be a plan for what they will do after Year 2000. Nobody expects that all Y2K effort will stop in the first three months of 2000, but it will diminish gradually and the programmers must have replacement work or must be let go at significant cost to the organisation.

Hiring contract programmers on an 'as needs' basis is superficially attractive but such people may have less loyalty and attachment to the organisation than the 'permanent' staff. They may leave, or cause friction with 'permanent' staff who are paid less. Attempts can be made to retain contract staff by agreeing Y2K completion bonuses (or penalties!). In parallel, 'permanent' staff may be offered benefits or extra pay to keep them competitive in remuneration terms with the contractors. With 'permanent' staff working on Y2K, it is also necessary to prepare them, with training in new technologies, for life in a post-Y2K world.

The third option is to bring back the older programmers. This approach may have a number of advantages. Such programmers may be able to work part-time, possibly from home. If they are ex-employees, they may have a loyalty lacking in contract staff. They are less likely to *need* the money they get for Y2K work; they may therefore be less expensive.

Many organisations, in order to get a dispassionate, knowledgeable, view on their Y2K problem, decide to engage one or more independent Y2K consultants. In deciding whether or not to hire a given consultant or firm, you should consider these questions:

- Is your project large and complex enough to benefit from a consultant's previously-gained experience?

- What Y2K projects has the consultant previously worked on?

- Has the consultant worked on large projects? Implementing a fix for 1,000 PCs or programs is very different from doing so for 10.

- Will the consultant guarantee the work and indemnify against failure?
- Does the consultant over-sell, perhaps promising to fix ALL your Y2K problems?
- How soon can the consultant start?
- How much will the consultant cost?
- Is the consultant just in it for the money?

Hiring a consultant can give the benefit of an objective unemotional view from a person unconnected with your organisation's internal 'politics'. In a large Y2K project particularly, experience gained on previous large projects can be of benefit. But beware: as I have pointed out, Y2K is not technically difficult, and there are plenty of opportunists in the market.

2.5 Small businesses

Most large businesses – banks, multinationals, governments – by now have a 'handle' on the Y2K problem, even if they have by no means yet solved it. But the great majority of businesses are of small-to-medium size, and it is here where the greatest problem of awareness arises and where, in fact, most of the global Y2K problem may manifest itself.

If a small business conducts electronic transactions from its computer systems to suppliers, clients or banks, it is at risk of transmitting to any of them non-Y2K-compliant data. For example, if it outsources its payroll function and, suddenly, the input data does not have the date format required by the payroll processing function, the business has a major problem. The business will also encounter problems if it sends wrong invoices or reminders to clients or fails to place orders with suppliers.

Many small businesses work with major institutional clients – banks, multinationals, governments again – who will require evidence of effort to implement Y2K compliance, impose Y2K compliance requirements on the business and expect written statements of compliance. There is clearly a major risk for the small business of losing the work with such clients if they fail to examine and fix the data they transmit according to the clients' specifications.

Many small businesses rely completely on packaged software running on PC networks. In large-scale client/server terms, they have no servers and, hence, no self-written application software to worry about. Their Y2K problem is therefore smaller and more tractable than that of major organisations, being confined to PCs, PC applications and the data they generate. The small business should assess the liability of their hardware and software suppliers to provide upgrades, perhaps free of charge, as well as considering the other legal points raised in this chapter.

The most important thing for the small business in the Y2K context is to address the problem, to learn about its possible effects and *not* to take the 'ostrich approach'. Fixing the Y2K problem may be simple – it may even not exist at all – but prudence dictates that it must be addressed. If in doubt as to where to start, a small business is well advised to engage an outside consultant for a few days, just to get a 'handle' on the problem and set up a project charged with resolving it. Once a plan is in place, it must be managed to conclusion, which should be well before 31 December 1999.

The technical fix for the small business may be to upgrade PC operating system and application software, as well as checking the format of data electronically exchanged. If there are fewer than about 50 PCs, the strategies for updating clients over a network, considered in later chapters, do not apply. Even if the problem is relatively easy to fix, it is vital that the business makes its 'effort and intent' clear to major clients and provides written statements of compliance.

2.6 System components

In considering Y2K, there is a tendency to over-emphasise certain aspects of the problem, at the expense of other, less-obvious, considerations. This is why so much attention seems to be focused on mainframe-centric application software written in COBOL or RPG; and on the behaviour of PC BIOSs when the clock ticks past midnight on 31 December 1999.

There is a famous aphorism in computing that *the system is the network*. This is true and, if applied, helps lead to the solution to almost any systems problem. Earlier in this chapter, I use the components of a typical client/server system to help decide what kind of technical representatives should be on the Y2K project team. We can further use this component approach to decide where the fixes must be applied. The overall problem is divided into two parts: Chapter 4, 'Fixing the Infrastructure', meaning the network, the component systems and operating system software; and Chapter 5, 'Fixing Applications', referring to the application programs that run on the infrastructure.

This component-driven, divide-and-conquer, approach is at the heart of putting together a realistic and achievable project plan. The diagram in Figure 2.1 is of a rather idealised network environment. What matters is that it depicts most, if not all, of the components of the system that must be repaired. It also expresses the interactions – exchange of data – that regularly occur with other departments in the organisation as well as with outside companies.

The environment comprises a host system with a 'back-end' database, a Local Area Network server, various kinds of client terminals, some peripheral devices and a network connecting all the parts together.

The host could be a mainframe, a UNIX or Windows NT/2000 server or, say, an Alpha-based system running OpenVMS. The clients include PCs, connected directly and via a hub as well as remote dumb terminals connected through a terminal server.

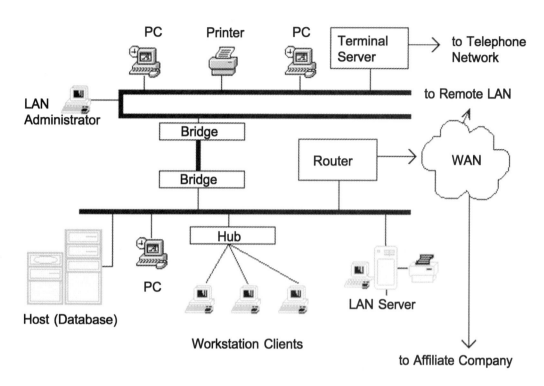

Figure 2.1 Typical LAN environment

The local LAN is bridged, and there are routers to connect it across a Wide Area Network (WAN) to a remote LAN in the same organisation and to the network of a separate company.

The alternative to the client/server LAN/WAN environment is the mainframe-based system depicted in the diagram (Figure 2.2).

The main difference between the client/server and the mainframe system is that the latter is more centralised; it handles almost all processing, and the terminals (Physical Units(PU), probably 3270s) run Logical Unit (LU) software to display the interaction between the user and the mainframe application programs.

On mainframe systems, the main focus of Y2K concern is indeed the centralised application software which users access using remote

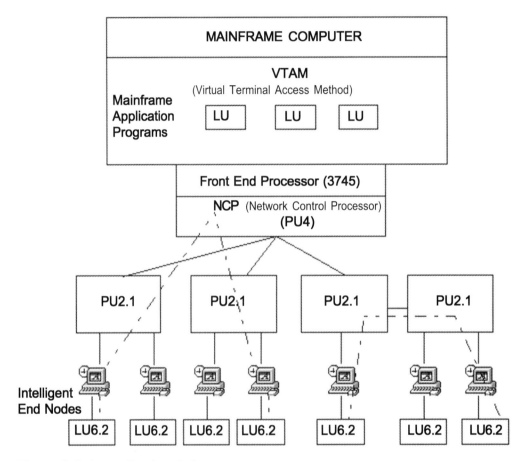

Figure 2.2 Centralised mainframe system

terminals. A secondary consideration is that displays presented to the user may have to be changed to accommodate expanded data information.

In the distributed client/server system, we have rather more to consider, under the headings:

- Clients: PC BIOS
- Clients: PC operating systems
- Clients: PC shrink-wrapped application software

- Clients: front-end client/server application software
- Network: date-dependent network software
- Servers: operating system compliance
- Servers: date-dependent application software and data
- External: incoming or outgoing data with incompatible date representation
- System management: deployment of new and repaired applications to servers and remote clients

The process of backing up and keeping security copies of data is vital on any system as a preliminary to implementing Y2K changes. In the distributed environment, backups are just as crucial and must be done for every type of system in the environment.

Ensuring that your system is Y2K-clean under these broad headings is the focus of Chapters 4 to 6. Before that, however, we take the recommendations of this chapter and apply them to the formulation of a year 2000 project plan.

3 | The Y2K project plan

3.1 Project prerequisites

The overall Y2K test plan must consider all the issues raised under the section headings of this chapter. I use the usually-redundant word 'overall' advisedly; there will be separate and subordinate plans defining the work to be done to apply the Y2K repairs, the necessary testing procedures and the process for migration to new or repaired applications.

Before proceeding to set down plans for doing the actual Y2K repair work, a number of prerequisite items must be in place, themselves a preliminary part of the project plan.

Awareness

The the networked, client/server, system in Figure 2.1 showed that the Y2K problem affects all parts of the organisation. Raising awareness of this fact is one of the main prerequisites for a successful repair project.

Most people know that some sort of a date 'bomb' is, if no remedial action is taken, going to affect the operation of centralised software systems such as payroll and stock-control. In a wider context, jokes abound about not flying on New Year's Day, 2000. They need to be aware that Y2K will touch them too, whatever part of the computer system they work with.

It is important to mount an awareness campaign throughout the organisation which highlights the consequences of what will happen if everyone does not play their part, back up their systems and co-operate with the project team. Applications will fail on the central system; some PCs will 'die' when the date changes; there will be network failures; data exchanges with clients and suppliers could fail, with consequences of varying seriousness. The key to success is in persuading individuals to *take ownership of*, and responsibility for, the part of the system they use.

Management support

At the technical level, Y2K is simple: does 75 mean 1975 or 2075; and is the year 00 a leap-year or not? Files with date information and the code to process them are everywhere, so date-dependencies affect all parts of the system. This makes Y2K primarily a business-process and management-level problem, not a technical one.

Management at the highest level must sponsor the Y2K project, giving it the highest priority. As evidence that it has this priority in some major organisations, it is increasingly the case, in banking and insurance in particular, that their IT departments are now focused almost totally on Y2K, with all other procurement decisions either on the 'back-burner' or deferred altogether until mid-2000 at the earliest.

Highest management must make clear to all parts of the organisation the seriousness of the problem and its commitment to solving it. Sign-off for procurement of all new hardware and software will be conditional on its being Y2K-compliant. PC users must sign-off that they have co-operated with the project team in applying BIOS fixes and otherwise checking the Y2K compliance of their workstations. Managers of different parts of the computer system – clients, network, servers – must be required to give regular reports to management, stating progress and signing-off on applications and hardware that have been made Y2K-compliant and unit-tested.

The manager responsible for system testing (testing many components together) must sign-off on the successful functioning of whole subsystems. For example, a client PC and its software is 'clean', so is the network and so, we believe, is the 'back-end' server application program. But does the whole lot work together? Can all the different types of transactions be done between client and server? The test manager must sign-off in the affirmative.

Individual users as well as Y2K project team members will be expected to take responsibility in this way for their parts of the system. In addition, management must ensure that the project team is 'in the loop' for wider decision-making: all decisions and changes made by the organisation in the run-up to 2000 must be signed off by the Y2K project manager. For example, before the organisation engages a new supplier, that supplier must state and demonstrate Y2K compliance according to our specification. It must be a requirement imposed by management that business cannot begin with the supplier until this compliance has been signed off as part of the Y2K project.

With this level of management commitment needed, it is ideal if the Y2K project manager is also a senior management executive. Y2K is expensive and budget sign-off authority is required; this is a further reason for including management on the project team. No project – not just a Y2K project – is more likely to fail than one for which responsibility is assigned to a manager without the budgetary authority to make it work.

Y2K project team

At least the central part of this team – project manager, legal representative, technical managers responsible for major subsystems – must be in place at the inception of the Y2K project. It is possible to co-opt from other parts of the organisation or hire consultants, programmers and technicians on an 'as needs' basis during the course of the project.

As we have already seen, the project manager should be a senior executive and the project should be centralised with cross-departmental responsibility. Users, supplier and clients may be represented on the project team or, in the case of the last two, at least consulted extensively.

Budget

Nothing happens without money. A decisive aspect of management commitment to the success of the Y2K project is its allocation of enough money to it, as well as delegation of authority to spend that money to the Y2K project manager. Chapter 2 makes an extensive listing of likely Y2K-related cost items. To the cost of new hardware, software and staff can be added the cost of inevitable overtime, particularly for the test function. This is less high-profile than the programming work of repairing applications but may in fact account for the majority of project activity.

No plan accurately foresees everything. Management must therefore commit to periodically reviewing – and augmenting, if necessary – the budget as the project progresses.

3.2 Inventory

Knowing the extent of what must be fixed – 'drawing a line around the problem' – is at the basis of every Y2K project plan. Only with this information concerning what hardware, software and data flow exist in your organisation, can you possibly make an assessment of what can be repaired in the time available. This section uses the model of a distributed system such as that presented at the end of Chapter 2 to guide you in building an inventory list. This list will then, in effect, drive your Y2K project.

The project team must devise a plan for how an inventory, or audit, of the entire computing environment, hardware and software, will be done. This is not a trivial task. In any large – or even small – organisation, who really *knows* what PCs are out there and with what BIOS levels? What applications do they run? Are all these applications known to and under the control of the IS department? Do individual PC users run database programs locally for their private use? What shrink-wrapped and home-grown application software is on the PCs? What applications are on the servers? Do we have all the source code? The list goes on, and its difficulty may be compounded by the problem of scalability: the information may be easy to get for 20 PCs or 20 mainframe-based applications, but what if the number becomes 200 or 2,000? The answer to the inventory problem lies in having both end-user co-operation and some software tools to aid in enumerating the organisation's assets.

Users can be asked to fill a questionnaire – we assume they are honest! – giving details of what PC they use and what software they know to be on it. Client operating systems such as Windows NT/ 2000 allow remote access from administrator systems to client PCs for purposes of inspection. Products such as PC Anywhere, from Symantec Corp., provide extensive capabilities for 'looking into' a remote PC from a central administrative site. There are fully-fledged systems management software tools that have inventory-taking capabilities – IBM's Tivoli; Computer Associates' UniCenter; Amdahl's Enterprise Desktop Manager; Microsoft's SMS. There are also PC audit software products, such as Viasoft's On Mark 2000 (see Chapter 7), which can find out what is on a PC. However, because of time pressure, the range of problems to be addressed, and the scalability problem inherent in hundreds or thousands of PCs, many organisations choose to take a minimalist approach: fix the BIOS on client PCs and otherwise let the problem 'look after itself'.

At the end of Chapter 2, there is a list of system components, based on the distributed client/server architecture:

- Clients: PC BIOS
- Clients: PC operating systems
- Clients: PC shrink-wrapped application software
- Clients: front-end client/server application software
- Network: date-dependent network software
- Server: operating system compliance

- Server: date-dependent application software and data
- External: incoming or outgoing data with incompatible date representation

I have left out the system management item: the issues of how to migrate to changed applications are covered in Chapter 6. The rest of this section considers each of the other items separately, summarising the activities necessary under each heading to effect the Y2K repair. In reality, few organisations go through the full range of these activities. They assess the impact of failures in various parts of the system, assign priorities and compromise on the extent of the repairs they will undertake. This process of rationalisation is considered in the section 3.3 (Assessment). For now, I enumerate a reasonably comprehensive list of potential inventory items, which you should use as a guide in building your organisation's inventory list.

Clients: PC BIOS

The first step in checking your organisation's PCs is to identify and locate them all. Surprisingly, this may not be as simple as it sounds, particularly in a large distributed system. Over time, PCs are moved to different locations on the network or are disconnected. Software tools exist which can 'see' all connected PCs, but those that are not connected to the network can be a problem to locate. The PC list will be drawn up based on address information to be found in the network configuration, the network administrator's knowledge and the user-supplied questionnaire. Assuming the list to be complete, or nearly so, the first item to be checked on each PC is the BIOS, which governs the PC's system date.

Either the BIOS in a PC can handle multiple centuries or it cannot. If it cannot, you really have no option but to replace the PC. If it can, either everything is fine or the BIOS needs a little programming. You can be fairly certain that Pentium-processor PCs supplied from 1996 onward have BIOSs capable of handling the century-change.

Some BIOSs have the capacity but need to be reprogrammed to deal with the change.

There are many programs commercially available – most on the Web – that check BIOSs for Y2K compliance. A (free) example is Test2000.exe, from the RighTime Company. To apply any such program to all the PCs in the organisation is no small task. Broadly, there are three options:

- A technician visits every PC and loads and runs the BIOS program

- The program is run on each PC from LAN servers. It must first be loaded to all the LAN servers.

- A software-distribution tool such as Microsoft's SMS is used to deploy the program to all the PCs, where it is then run.

Perhaps surprisingly, the first of these options is the most common. Although it has the old problem of scalability – visiting each of possibly thousands of PCs – there is one major advantage over the other two approaches. This is that the BIOS check is done in person by a qualified technician rather than the end user. The direct-visit approach is the most common probably because system and network administrators deeply dislike the thought of naïve users running sensitive utilities to check (and possibly change) their BIOSs. BIOS details, along with the necessary checks and changes, are covered in Chapter 4.

Clients: PC operating systems

Typical Intel PCs may run any of five major operating systems: DOS, Windows 3.x, Windows 95/98, Windows NT/2000 and IBM's OS/2 Version 4. To complicate the picture, each of these can run in many variants with many fix, or 'service', levels. Back-versions may be running: there is still a huge installed base of Microsoft Windows 3.1 and, in IBM installations especially, of OS/2 Version 3 (Warp).

To find what operating systems are currently running on your organisation's PCs, you must either know, or find out from the user questionnaire or by using an audit tool. In either case, an addition to the inventory software list is the result. Many organisations have standardised on a common desktop operating environment such as Windows NT/2000. On the other hand, there are many which run a variety of operating systems and who are intending to use the Y2K necessity as an 'excuse' to migrate to a standard.

You can really only count on Windows 98, Windows NT/2000 and OS/2 Version 4 to be Y2K-clean. Late versions of Windows 95 are compliant, but MS-DOS and Windows 3.x are not. IBM's PC-DOS – almost identical to MS-DOS – is compliant and may be considered as an alternative. More details of operating-system tests and repair approaches are given in Chapter 4.

Clients: PC shrink-wrapped application software

If a shrink-wrapped PC application program – examples include Microsoft Word, Lotus 1-2-3, and any email tool – does not handle dates before and after the change to January 1, 2000, it must be replaced. There are software tools to enumerate PC applications and to determine whether or not they are ready for Year 2000. There are also various manual means of checking for the same thing; again, there is more on this in Chapter 4. Current versions of most major applications appear to be Y2K-clean. Upgrading desktop applications on a large number of PCs is itself a challenge. You should check for availability of free Y2K upgrades or patches before going and paying the full licence price for the replacement.

Clients: front-end client/server application software

Your organisation may have PC applications, most likely the front-end of a client/server program, written or tailored to its specification. While you could use a software tool to search for these, you really should know what applications are specific to your organisation. This information should in any case be contained in the user questionnaire.

If the application came from a third-party supplier, you are in an upgrade situation similar to the one applying to shrink-wrapped applications. Because the application is not mass-market and was at least partly tailored for your organisation, you may have more influence in getting an upgrade.

If the program was written in-house in your organisation, the repair approach is similar to that adopted for self-written server applications.

Network: date-dependent network software

There are two considerations here: the network software in use on a given computer and the network operating system (NOS) on the LAN to which a client is connected.

Network software comprises either the 'stack' (often an implementation of TCP/IP) resident on both client and server or programs that control routers and gateways. Usually, these days, the 'stacks' are supplied as an integral part of the client or server operating system. If the OS is Y2K-clean, the 'stack' is likely to be also. In the case of routers and gateways, there are probably not huge numbers of them in your organisation and so they are easy to enumerate; the test is to see if they can handle files with post-1999 dates.

The NOS runs on a network server. This is distinct from the term 'server' used to mean a computer running a 'back-end' database application that responds to requests from client PCs – an 'application server'. Normally, a client PC references its own resources, such as the C: drive. If the client requests access to the 'mapped' drive K:, this request is passed on to the NOS. The NOS then finds the mapped drive and gives the client the illusion that the drive is local to the client. The most common NOSs are Novell NetWare and Windows NT Server.

If a PC takes its system date from the network server and if that server is not Y2K-compliant, the PC will have the Y2K problem even though its own BIOS is clean. Therefore, all network servers must be added to the inventory list for later inspection.

Server: operating system compliance

Server operating systems are usually one of MVS (particularly in the centralised, mainframe, model, also called OS/390), UNIX, OpenVMS or Windows NT/2000. Up-to-date versions of these are all Y2K-compliant; the only risk arises if an old version of a minicomputer or a mainframe OS is in use. Any administrator will know all the server operating systems in use and where they are running. This is an easy part of the inventory process.

Server: date-dependent application software and data

This is the part most enterprises concentrate on: how many applications are running on a server or mainframe system, what files are in use and is the combination Y2K-clean? These are the so-called 'mission-critical' applications, which explains why they get the limelight.

A typical mainframe system may have a suite of many hundreds of applications using thousands of files. These can be fixed, but the problem of scalability hits hard here: how many COBOL (or RPG or PL/1 or Assembler) programmers will be needed to check and fix all the code?

There are software tools, particularly for mainframes, which not only enumerate the applications in use but also generate dependency lists containing information on the files the applications use, the software libraries they call and the source code modules from which the applications were generated. The concentration of available tools is highest in this area, which reflects the fact that the applications are centralised and accessible and that there are vast amounts of code to check. The formats of files and database tables in use must also be determined, along with screen layouts used to display the data they contain. Both files and screen layouts commonly have date-dependencies.

It is not difficult at least to enumerate the server or mainframe applications that are in use; how to fix them is the subject of Chapter 5.

External: incoming and outgoing data

There is no automatic way of identifying data sent and received. You must enumerate all suppliers and clients, identify and list the files and other data transferred regularly, and arrange a specification agreed with the third party to ensure that the data is usable by both sides.

3.3 Assessment

The process of assessment consists of identifying which items of hardware and software found by the inventory process are both affected by the Y2K problem and are 'mission-critical'; and which are either unaffected or can be repaired later. The assessment process considers software more than hardware and in particular concentrates on application software developed specially for the organisation, either in-house or by an outside supplier. In a centralised mainframe system, the application is entirely mainframe-resident. In a client/server environment, part of the application is on the client and part on the server. Either way, the whole application must be assessed.

We take the output of the inventory process and consider the application programs, their files and the user interface they present. There are two types of application: those that are affected by Year 2000 (the majority) and those that are not. The applications not affected are in the first instance probably suspected by those familiar with the overall application suite; they can be confirmed as non-Y2K-dependent by examining their inputs and outputs. After this confirmation is made, no further attention is paid to these applications in the context of the Y2K project.

The set of Y2K-affected applications is again divided in two categories: those that are 'mission-critical' and those that are not. The 'mission-critical' applications – those whose correct functioning is vital to keep the organisation in business – are obviously fixed first. The others will be fixed later or perhaps not at all, if the project team considers that the problems they may cause can be lived with or if there simply is not enough time.

A given 'mission-critical' application must be examined in a series of steps:

- All source code must be scanned, first by a software tool, for date-dependencies; all dependencies found must be listed and categorised.

- All source code must be manually checked for more dependencies. A scanning tool may be 95% or 99% accurate in its 'crawl' through the source code. This is not good enough: none is guaranteed to be 100% accurate, so a manual check is a necessity. Further dependencies found are also listed and categorised.

- Source code of all libraries – utility software – used by the application must also be scanned and checked.

- All input and output files must be checked for date-dependency, and all dependencies listed.

- These files include all files received from outside organisations that will be used as input to the application and all files generated by the application that will be sent to any outside party.

- All database tables and indexes used by the application must be checked for date-dependency.

- Stored procedures in any database used by the application must be examined.

- Files output from this application and used as the input to another must be modified to be of the format required by the other application.

- Input and output screen layouts which are used by the application and contain date-dependencies must also be changed, along with the code and data 'behind' them.

When the results of this exhaustive examination are tabulated, we have the input to the work plan (see The Work Plan, section 3.4) for that application. The same procedure must be applied for all 'mission-critical' applications.

Date classification

The term 'date-dependency' means in general any date processing, performed by the application, which assumes the wrong century and generates an error as a consequence. It can be refined into a more accurate classification:

- Dates which span more than 100 years but in which the year is represented by only two year-digits and which are processed by code sensitive to the current date. For example, does '50' mean a 1950 or 2050 Government bond issue? I refer to these as Class 1 dates. They are the most 'expensive' dates to be fixed for Y2K, as file formats and data representations must be changed to show four-digit years explicitly.

- Dates referring to events a short distance in the past or future which imply the century they are part of: if my mortgage matures on 06/06/03, I know that '03' represents 2003 and not 1903. I refer to these as Class 2 dates. These dates can be fixed for Y2K in program logic only; file formats and data representations need not be changed.

- Dates which are already Year 2000-ready and for which no modification need be made to the application or its files. Examples include dates already stored with four-digit years, dates which are entered to the program and then not used and dates appear on reports or displays where neither sorting nor ordering of the dates is required. I refer to these as Class 3 dates.

This is the lowest level of program assessment short of actually applying the Y2K repair. In classifying the dates in the way shown, the amount of repair work is minimised: no work need be done for Class 3 dates; Class 2 dates can be fixed in program logic only; and only Class 1 dates require change in file formats. These low-level dependencies identified can be added to the list of required changes for the application and input to the work plan, referred to above. However, documenting micro-changes in this way and assigning them individually to people to fix will produce a very long list and a very long schedule. It is most important to identify in the application the three relevant kinds of dates — those in files, on screens and in code – and to schedule these into the work plan along with their classification.

Third-party software

Application software developed to the specification of your organisation by an outside supplier must be subject to the same assessment process. The difficulty is that someone else developed the code and your organisation may not have internal knowledge of how it works or what files it uses. Also, you may not have access to the source code of the application, in which case you depend on the supplier to fix the application or to give you the source code.

Assuming a given third-party application to be 'mission-critical', the options open to your organisation are these:

- Agree with the original supplier (if they are still in business) that they will Y2K-fix the software.

- Get the source code and repair the application within your organisation.

- Rewrite the application.

- Outsource an alternative application.

None of these options is easy. If the original supplier still exists and can reliably fix the application, it is convenient but may be expensive. If there are any interfaces - files or databases - between the application and any of your organisation's other programs, these must be specified to the supplier so that the application will continue to work in your environment.

It is unlikely that the supplier will be willing to release the source code for your organisation to modify. If they do and if you modify, there is a question over whether or not the supplier will continue to provide support for the modified application. Any updates subsequently released by the supplier probably will not be applicable to your modified version. Then there is the effort actually to do the work; it will place further strain on your already stretched Y2K team.

A full rewrite under the pressure of the approaching Year 2000 is not something most IS managers would willingly contemplate but, if all other options fail and if the application is indeed 'mission-critical', it may have to be considered.

Outsourcing an alternative application seems attractive if there is one available that closely matches requirements. Even then, however, data will have to be transferred between the old and new files. In a surprising proportion of cases, the quickest way to do this is by manual re-entry, with all its attendant scope for error (and expense).

The only advice in the case of applying Y2K repairs to third-party applications is to take whichever of the above options seems most reliable and least expensive in your circumstances.

Assigning priorities

In designating certain applications 'mission-critical', we have already assigned an important priority – or made an important compromise, depending on your view. These applications will receive the Y2K repair treatment first and the rest will follow if there is time. Experience shows, however, that anything which it is not absolutely necessary to do, and which is put 'on the long finger', will end up not getting done.

Therefore, the definition of 'mission-critical' should not be too tight. Some applications, and the way they work, may not be quite 'mission-critical' but are still important enough that their failure may adversely affect your business. For example, if a report is sequenced wrongly on date or 10,000 bills are printed in an unexpected order, the system can still be said to be 'working' but tell that to the individual who must search and sort among the 10,000 bills! In short, the Y2K repair should be applied on the basis of it being prudent to do so and not just unavoidable.

If, in a distributed client/server system the proportions of the Y2K repair project are considered according to the components of the system, it turns out that the proportion of change on the client side is actually in a majority. Experiences will differ but perhaps 65% of the total change is needed to Y2K-clean large numbers of workstations, 5–10% for the network and the remainder for the 'back-end', server-resident applications. In light of this, the greatest compromise is the most common one: many organisations only make BIOS fixes on client PCs. Centralised remote update of operating systems and applications to the PCs is eliminated. Keeping the clients functional is left to the 'user community' (for which read local PC administrators) to do on an ad-hoc basis.

Apart from all but ignoring the client side of the system, the most effective assignment of priorities is that of classifying dates as shown above. If the Y2K project team takes an application program and expands all dates regardless of whether they are of Class 1, 2 or 3, the Y2K fix will prove very inefficient. The application will also be changed to a much greater extent – perhaps by a factor of 10 – than is necessary. The scope for error is multiplied accordingly, as is the amount of testing that will be required.

There is one upside to all of this: the inventory and assessment processes may yield information on systems and applications that are lightly used, if at all. Output reports may never be read and a Y2K failure might not be noticed until well after January 1, 2000. Where this turns out to be the case, the application should be quietly retired. Any freed-up space or system capacity can be regarded as a beneficent side-effect of the Y2K effort.

3.4 Work plan

The next step uses the output of the inventory and assessment procedures to produce a detailed and specific work plan. This is a fully-fledged project plan for the 'repair' part of the Y2K project. Like every project plan, it is a list of steps and activities that must be executed to achieve the goal required of the project – in this case ensuring that at least the critical parts of the computing environment will not fail when the date changes to 2000.

A work plan is characterised by being detailed, specific and time-limited. Tasks are assigned to people who then have responsibility for their completion within the time specified. Critical paths – for example, identification and acquisition of a Y2K source-code scanning tool – are identified, and budget availability is ensured so that other activities are not held up.

The work plan and its activities are based on information found during the inventory and assessment phases. There follows a summary listing of activities that might be found in a work plan. Time allowances for each activity will be specific to your organisation, so no attempt is made to estimate them here. Once again, the list is organised by system component.

Clients: PC BIOS

The inventory phase will have determined which of the organisation's PCs are Y2K-compliant. The work plan must address the others with these steps:

- Ensure that all PC users back up valuable data stored locally.

- For all PCs with BIOSs capable of being reprogrammed to take multiple centuries, arrange to have the 'fix' program executed.

- This will either involve visiting each PC or remotely executing the 'fix' program.

- For all PCs with non-Y2K-compliant BIOSs either upgrade the BIOS or decide on replacement.

- For all replaced PCs, initialise the operating system.

- Connect replaced PCs to the network and configure them.

- Install required applications on replaced PCs.

Replaced PCs will usually be initialised, network-configured and set up with applications at a central administrator location before being dispatched to their final network locations. The administrator may initialise the PC from a disk image common to PCs throughout the organisation. The disk image (also called the *gold build*) will contain operating system, network configuration and all applications. The alternative, replacing the BIOS on the old PC, raises questions of compatibility and support that the administrator may choose to avoid by replacement.

Clients: PC operating systems

The inventory process will have decided which of the organisation's PCs runs a non-Y2K-compliant operating system. It may also report on obsolete operating systems, for example identifying all instances of Windows 3.x where the policy is to upgrade all clients to Windows NT/2000.

Upgrading client operating systems is a major undertaking. Many organisations are taking advantage of the need for Y2K repair on client PCs by upgrading the PC operating systems at the same time. There are three broad approaches (I expand on these in Chapter 4), the first two involving the 'burn and build' step:

- Initialise each PC, either at its network location or centrally, with the gold build.

- Initialise each PC at its network location, using a 'boot diskette' configured with network software to download the gold build files over the network.

- On each PC, at its network location, manually reinstall the operating system, network software and applications.

All of the approaches will cause application data stored locally to be erased. It is the PC user's responsibility to have backed up the data.

In common practice, the first option is probably the most typically taken, with network installation less so. Manual reinstallation is only practical if the number of PCs is small: you can do it for 20 but not for 2,000. Whichever of the options you choose, a list of activities to implement it must be included in the work plan. If your organisation chooses the gold-build approach, plan for the following implementation steps:

- Based on the output of the inventory and assessment phases, list all client system and application software in use throughout the organisation.

- Decide whether or not one common set of software can be deployed to all client PCs in the organisation.

- If more than one set is required – for different application requirements, or system software such as device drivers – define how many this number is.

- List and document the components of all the software sets, declaring the content of each gold build.

- Define the content of boot diskettes to be used.

- Estimate when the gold builds can actually be assembled, allowing for the availability of Y2K-compliant operating system, software utilities and applications (both home-grown and shrink-wrapped). This estimation, and its reliability, is critical to the success of the client side of the Y2K project.

- Decide whether the gold-build installation of individual PCs will be done at the PCs' end-user location or centrally.

- Whatever the choice, agree an installation plan with end-users.

- Schedule groups of PCs for reinstallation.

Clients: PC shrink-wrapped application software

Standard mass-market application software may have to be replaced on client PCs with Y2K-compliant versions. There are four approaches to doing this after procuring the new version(s) of the application software:

- At its network location, manually install the application software on each PC.

- Install the application software on the network server of each client PC and run it from there.

- Use a software-deployment tool to load the application software to each client PC over the network.

- Include the application software in the gold build and initialise the PC.

The first option is made impractical where PC numbers are large. The second is better, but at the price of increased network traffic generated in running application software from network servers. The third is complex, requiring familiarity with and mastery of the software-deployment tool. The last needs very good planning and co-ordination with those responsible for the other components – system software and applications – of the build. Despite this, the gold-build approach offers a clean and comprehensive solution to the problem of updating client PCs and many organisations devote a great deal of effort to it. The content of the build is updated periodically with the latest operating system and applications and, when updated, a PC is always initialised. This approach can be tied in well with applying Y2K software fixes to client PCs, and is currently prevalent in large enterprises.

Clients: front-end client/server application software

The steps for applying on client PCs Y2K-fixed front-end software are these:

- Check and fix the software according to the steps specified for server software below.

- Install the Y2K-compliant version to all Client PCs either manually, over the network or as part of a gold build.

Again, the gold-build reinstallation approach is the most comprehensive and commonly used in large organisations.

Network: date-dependent network software

The problem here is either in the 'stack' of network software supplied integrally with most modern operating systems, or with the NOS on a network server, or both. In either case, you are dealing with system software which must be replaced. These are the steps to be planned for:

- If the 'stack' is to be updated, procure the update either as a new version of the operating system or as part of a 'service pack' (manufacturer's fix).

- Apply the updated 'stack' to all clients, probably by incorporating it in the gold build.

- Procure an updated Y2K-compliant version of the NOS.

- Install the NOS manually to all network servers.

- Consider also the case of client PCs connected to more than one network server and NOS. There may be a conflict here in which of multiple servers' dates (perhaps not Y2K-compliant) a PC will synchronise with.

Server: operating system compliance

If the operating system, such as MVS or OpenVMS, running on an application server, is not Y2K-compliant, it must be reinstalled manually, probably along with the applications which run on that server. It is vital, before reinstalling, to take comprehensive backups of application software and data.

Server: date-dependent application software and data

All application software developed in-house should, by the time the work plan is being formulated, have been identified as an inventory item and then analysed as part of the assessment procedure. The outputs of the assessment determine, for a given application, the specific work tasks needed to fix it.

Here is the list of specific steps to be taken in fixing an application:

- Consider the list output from the analysis of the application done at the assessment phase.
- Create test scripts for unit-test of the application.
- Create the test environment.
- Apply Class 1 date (expansion) changes to files and database tables.
- Apply Class 1 date changes to source code.
- Apply Class 1 date changes to screen definitions.
- Apply Class 2 date changes to source code.
- Make no change to Class 3 dates.
- Compile the programs.
- Fix and recompile any necessary library programs used by the application.
- Unit test the application.
- If necessary, make changes and repeat.

The details of these steps are the subject of Chapter 5. Note the distinction between the different classes of dates; this is a key element in reducing the extent of the work to be done – code change and testing – in repairing the application.

External: incoming and outgoing data

The difficulty here is one of co-ordination. The assessment phase will have identified down to the field level, Class 1 and Class 2 dates within files being exchanged with suppliers and clients. A task must be included in the work plan and assigned to an analyst to agree with all third parties the format of all dates stored on exchanged files. The formats adopted will be influenced by the respective organisations' classification of dates and the way they process them. The processing methods – date expansion, date windowing, date encoding and date compression – are explored in Chapter 5.

It is unlikely that your organisation will choose to make all the above activities part of its Y2K project. For example, you may simply choose not to include updating client PCs within the scope of the Y2K project. Whatever approach you do adopt, the list by system component should serve as a checklist that you can use as a guideline.

3.5 Test plan

Any part of the computing environment, from mainframe application to client PC BIOS, to which a Y2K fix has been applied must be tested. Additionally, each system component that might be affected by the roll-over to 2000 must be tested, whether or not it has been modified itself. Each step in the test effort must be described beforehand in a test plan. The test plan will contain such items as estimates of the testing time required, preparation of test data and the different tests to be carried out.

The test-and-fix phase of any project, including Y2K, is often reckoned to account for a majority – 50%–60% is normal – of the project schedule. It is desirable to reduce the scope of Y2K changes made; the extent of testing is reduced proportionately. On the server side, if *all* dates in an application are Y2K-fixed when most do not need to be, a great deal of unnecessary testing will have to be done. For clients, centralised testing of a software environment guaranteed to be common to all, or a large body of, PCs in the organisation saves a lot of time that might otherwise be spent testing and fixing at individual PCs' end-user locations. Reducing the scope of Y2K changes is the key to reducing testing and the time and effort needed for the project as a whole.

Organisational

Before planning the test process itself, the people and resources that will be used to execute the testing work must be identified:

- Identify the people who will design, prepare and execute tests, both on the client and server sides of the system.

- Identify people to evaluate and document test results.

- Identify people responsible for sign-off at each stage of testing.

- Define sign-off and acceptance criteria.

- Identify parties responsible for accepting Y2K-repaired software and hardware.

- Acquire and configure test hardware in each of the categories client, network and server.

- Identify and ensure availability of all necessary Y2K tools and utilities.

- Define change-control procedures to ensure availability for the test of the latest version of the software being tested.

- Ensure that the right test data for that software is defined and available.

- Ensure that there are sufficient resources (e.g. disk space for multiple versions) on the test system.

- Agree with all interested parties when the testing work can be done. If, as is desirable, a completely off-line, independent, test environment is available, testing can be scheduled at will.

- Do everything possible to have end-users and their departments 'take ownership' of the Y2K implementation and testing as is it relevant to them. A major cause of failed projects is a 'not my problem' attitude on the part of those for whom the computer system is being implemented.

Client

The following items are key considerations in any plan for testing Y2K-compatible client PCs, both in hardware and software:

- Crucially, decide the mechanism your organisation will use for deploying Y2K-repaired system software and application software to client PCs. If PCs have software individually deployed to them in an ad-hoc manner, then in principle they will all need to be tested separately at their end-user locations. If a gold build approach, or other strategy for centralised uniform deployment, is used, testing can be centralised and proportionately reduced.

- Plan the composition of a client test environment. At the test site, there will need to be a PC representative of every configuration used in the organisation.

- Identify the people who will do the testing and assign responsibilities.

- Identify PC configurations on which BIOSs must be tested.

- Identify and acquire the required BIOS-checking programs to be used in testing.

- Schedule execution of BIOS and operating system tests.

- Specify date tests for the operating system; these will check how the operating system handles important post-1999 boundary dates.

- Specify tests for all PC applications with the same boundary dates, as well as window dates (see Chapter 5).

- For system testing of the client portion of client/server applications, specify a representative set of transactions and data to test co-operative processing with the server.

- Document these tests, along with the expected results.

- Plan test of the gold build, including successful running of applications and connection with server.

- Plan a multiple-PC test of the gold build.

- Schedule departmental acceptance tests.

Server

There is a school of thought that testing applications for Y2K-compliance is different from 'conventional' testing. The theory is that conventional testing largely involves verifying that new functionality works, while Y2K concentrates more on ensuring that changed software continues to work with existing system components. Test activities go by different titles in different organisations, but there are distinct phases, particularly for server-based application software, that are widely recognised:

- unit test

- integration test

- system test

- regression test

- acceptance test.

When an application program is written or modified, it is compiled and loaded into the form of an executable program or library. It is then unit-tested to verify as far as possible that it runs properly on its own.

Integration testing follows: the application may interact with a client, showing that it can work over the network and with other programs. System testing is like integration testing at a higher level: it ensures, for example, that a client/server application works between the PC and the application server, correctly producing pre-defined results. If the operating system on client or server were then upgraded, or if other applications were changed, a regression test would be needed to ensure that the results of all previous tests were still valid. (This is the area held to be more important for Y2K than conventional development projects). Finally, there is acceptance test, requiring the sign-off of the end-users.

Application software, when changed, must go through this series of tests but may have additional associated activities such as creation of test data. For every application software component that may be affected by Y2K repairs, entries must be made in the test plan under these headings:

- Estimate of length of test
- Identification of people and resources involved, including end-users
- Preparation of test data
- Definition of test procedure
- Preparation of test scripts
- Preparation of test environment
- Unit test
- Analysis of test output
- Documentation of test output
- Integration test
- System test
- Regression test
- Acceptance test.

Not all these steps apply in the same degree to all components in the system. Only components that have actually been changed need to be unit tested, for example. An application program that has not been changed can simply be part of the system and regression tests to ensure that it still functions alongside other applications and devices which have been repaired.

All entries in the test plan must have people assigned to the activity and an allotted time for its completion. Server applications should have entries in the plan under all headings.

3.6 Migration

When an application has been subjected to all the tests, it must somehow be placed in production – the process known as migration. Like everything else about the Y2K project, migration must be planned, and documented as part of a migration plan. General items that must be included in the migration plan include:

- Scheduling when the migration will be done.
- Co-ordinating this schedule with the actual availability of the software being migrated to.
- If migration to a new client build is at issue, it must be co-ordinated with availability of other Y2K-repaired desktop software, perhaps in gold build form.
- Assigning people to identified migration activities.
- Define post-migration sign-off and acceptance criteria.

Server

In a centralised mainframe environment, applications do not have to be deployed to many targets, as is the case with client PCs. Centralisation has its benefits here; when the application has been through its tests it can be placed in production quite quickly.

When doing the migration, distinction needs to be made between applications which need *bridges* and those which do not. Bridges are file conversion programs used to allow incompatible applications to share data from the same file. For example, a file containing expanded dates is to be accessed by a program that has not yet been repaired for Y2K. The program *needs only to read from the file*, to refer to non-expanded, YYMMDD, dates. Before this application is executed, a bridge program is run to make the required conversion from expanded dates stored on file to the non-expanded date format in memory, needed by the application.

Eventually, when all programs have been Y2K-repaired, the bridges will become obsolete. Or so the story goes; in fact, at least some bridge programs may be around indefinitely to avoid the need to carry out Y2K repairs on all programs.

In general, programs which process only Class 2 dates – those whose data formats are changed in program logic only and not on file – do not need bridges. They do not require expanded dates in the files they use. The files thus do not have to be converted and can remain in operation with older applications. After testing has been completed, such a program can be moved to production without further ado.

Programs that process Class 1 dates – those which are expanded on file and where the century information is used by the code – make bridges necessary. Older programs need the original, non-expanded, file format and this is what the bridge provides. Before moving into production programs that process Class 1 dates, a bridge must be available to allow other software to co-exist. Bridges are usually simple programs but entries must be made in the migration plan for the work involved in writing them, or acquiring them.

The following items will be major components of any migration plan for server hardware and software:

- Define the migration process: what sequence of steps must be effected to get to a functioning Y2K-ready server?
- Estimate time, resources and people needed for the migration.
- Assign people to identified migration activities.

- Identify all data the must be converted before changeover to the Y2K-clean system.

- Write programs or acquire utilities for automatic data conversion.

- Plan for manual re-entry of data that cannot be automatically converted.

- Identify applications that can continue to operate using bridge programs.

- Write or acquire any bridge programs needed.

- Identify requirements for new or enlarged hardware. The primary requirement is usually disk space for multiple versions of files and software, as well as backups of pre-Y2K applications and data.

- In consultation with system administrators and end-users, establish arrangements for actually deploying Y2K-ready applications and making them operational.

- Define any requirement for training end-users in the operation of migrated software, and schedule that training.

Client

Migration to new application versions on clients is much more difficult than on centralised servers. This is, again, because of scalability: there are at most a few servers but possibly thousands of clients. A Y2K-repaired client application can be installed to the client in any of three ways:

- Manually, on a visit by a technician to the client PC.

- Using a software tool such as Tivoli to deploy the application over the network to the client.

- By including the fixed application in the organisation's gold build and initialising the PC. As already noted, this may involve bringing the PC 'back to base' or deploying the gold build to the PC over the network.

The first option is simple but labour-intensive for large numbers of clients. In addition, there is no easy way of ensuring that the new application will go live on all PCs at the same time. If a client calls for support, the help-desk will have difficulty knowing which version of the application is in use.

Network deployment carries with it a whole range of difficulties, most seriously that of limited available bandwidth to transfer large applications and system images.

The most common way of doing client deployments is using the gold-

build approach, either centrally or at the PC's network location. Again, the challenge is that a great deal of planning, and testing prior to deployment, must go into organising a consistent Y2K-clean suite of operating system and applications for distribution to the clients.

4 | Fixing the infrastructure

4.1 Introduction

This chapter concentrates on the steps you need to take to apply Y2K repairs to your organisation's distributed client/server computing environment. At issue are client PCs; their BIOSs and operating systems; network software and network operating systems; and server operating systems. The mechanics of applying the Y2K fix to applications are dealt with in Chapter 5.

If you are concerned only with a centralised mainframe system, this chapter will be of relevance only for the server side of the equation. And, because updating the client side is so much more of a problem than the server, you are in fact spared many of the difficulties.

However, most computer systems these days contain at least an element of distribution and client/server applications. Relatively few are still purely mainframe-centric with SNA (IBM's System Network Architecture) links connecting 'green-screen' dumb terminals to a central mainframe.

Most Y2K books tend to concentrate on the procedures needed to repair centralised applications and to ignore, or go lightly on, the steps involved in upgrading large numbers of client PCs. Given the predominance of client/server implementations today, this approach is unrealistic.

As anyone planning Y2K repair, test and migration for a distributed system soon finds out, the bulk of the problem is on the client (PC) side. The steps in repairing mainframe or server-centred applications are quite well understood although detailed and complex enough in themselves. It is on the client side, though, that the scalability problem may even make a full Y2K repair impractical.

This chapter gives a summary of the steps involved in fixing the infrastructure for client, network and server.

4.2 Client system clock

For the Y2K upgrade, the client PC must be considered in terms of some of its constituent parts:

- CMOS/BIOS
- Operating system
- Network components.

CMOS/BIOS

The CMOS hardware-level real time clock (RTC) is located in a chip on the PC's motherboard and keeps track of the time and date, even when the machine is turned off. Only the last two digits of the year are stored with the month and day, for example 23 08 98. The century is stored in a separate single digit: '9' to represent the '19' of the 20th century; '0' to mean the 21st century. When the Year 2000 arrives, the part of the year stored with the month and date will roll over from 99 to 00, but the century digit may not roll from 19 to 20. Thus, the year will become 1900 rather than 2000. Many older (pre-1996) PCs are designed in this way. In a machine that is Y2K compliant, the century digit will change from '9' to '0'. If it does not, the machine is not compliant. Some older machines may have no century digit at all. These machines cannot be made Y2K compliant.

The BIOS communicates between the operating system and the computer's hardware. When the PC is started, the BIOS reads the information from the RTC stored in CMOS and interprets it. A BIOS that is Y2K-compliant will understand that the century must roll from 19 to 20. If the BIOS cannot correctly interpret the RTC – as, in many older computers, it cannot – it may have a so-called 'flash' BIOS that can accept a software upgrade. Updating the BIOS in this way is a complicated and risky process. If the BIOS cannot be upgraded, or if you do not wish to update the 'flash' BIOS, it may be possible to correct the problem through the operating system on the PC.

An operating system generally keeps its own date, but it gets that date from the BIOS (which has in turn read and interpreted the date from the RTC) when the PC starts. The operating system's date remains the machine's system date as long as the system is turned on, and the operating system can update the RTC via the BIOS. Because of this, some machines may roll over to the year 2000 correctly if they happen to be running at midnight on December 31, 1999, depending on the particular operating system being used, but they may not roll over properly if the machine is turned off at the rollover. For every client PC, we need to test whether or not:

- The CMOS can accommodate multiple centuries.
- If it can, the BIOS can interpret 2000 and later.
- The operating system can interpret 2000 and later dates.
- The date will roll from 1999 to 2000 with the PC switched off.

There are many available software utilities to perform these tests, with hundreds available on the Web alone. The manual (command-line) procedure is this:

- Disconnect any network connection to the PC (this is done because the NOS may impose a system date on the PC).
- Close down all running programs.
- Start a DOS prompt.
- Set the date to December 31 1999. Enter the command 'date' at the prompt, followed by 31-12-99, or 12-31-99 if the North American format is required.
- Set the time to 23:58. Run the command 'time' and enter 23:58.

- Leave the PC switched on and, three minutes later, verify (with the 'date' and 'time' commands) that the roll-over to 2000 has taken place.

- Once again, set the time to 31-12-99 and the time to 23:58. Now power down the PC.

- Three minutes later, start the PC.

- At a command line, check the date and time. Verify that 1999 has changed to 2000.

There are two date checks. In the first, the clock is allowed to proceed through midnight on December 31 1999 with the PC remaining switched on. In the second, the PC is powered off before the clock reaches midnight and is restarted afterwards. This is what the manual interaction for the first test looks like at a Windows 95 command-line:

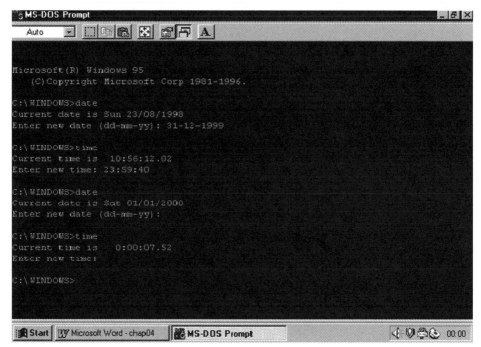

This test was successful. If both date-checks show a 2000 date and time, the PC's CMOS and BIOS are Y2K-compliant.

Control Panel

Some people prefer to use the equivalent GUI-based procedure for applying the date/time tests to a client PC. If the PC is running Windows 95/98 or Windows NT/2000, you start at the Control Panel, accessed from the 'My Computer' icon:

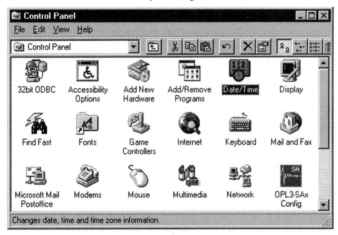

Selecting the Date/Time icon causes the following dialog box to appear:

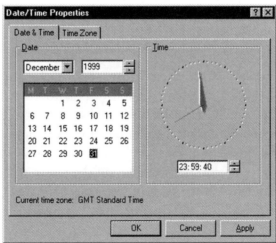

Note that the date and time have been set to December 31 1999, 20 seconds before the 'roll-over', in readiness for the change. The system clock is allowed to advance without further intervention. If the CMOS and BIOS are Y2K-compliant, the Date/Time display should end up looking like this:

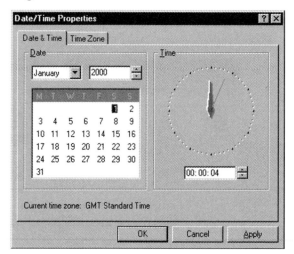

If one or both of the tests failed, either using the command-line or the GUI approach, the following options are open:

- The PC's BIOS may be capable of being 'flash'-upgraded.

- The BIOS can be physically replaced.

- The PC can be replaced with a Y2K-compliant model.

The last is the most drastic approach, but definitely the best. Upgraded PCs have a habit of not working. The downside is that the new PC must be initialised with your organisation's preferred operating system, communications and application environment - the 'gold build'. But, as I have noted, many organisations are taking the opportunity of upgrading their PCs to a common gold-build standard 'on the back of' the Year 2000 fix.

4.3 Client operating systems

Filesystem dates

The easiest way to check whether or not a PC operating system is Y2K-compliant is to create a file and write it to disk with the system date set to later than 23:59:59 on December 31 1999. In the Windows 95/98 and Windows NT/2000 environments, this can be done with any editor. If the system date is set to say, May 14, 2000, the datestamp of the file in either environment appears as 14/05/00 (assuming UK and not North American date settings are in force). In older operating environments, this date is displayed wrongly; in Windows 3.1, it appears as 14/05/:0. Even with the later Windows systems, only the two digits '00' – not 2000 – are displayed. Here is a technique that will verify that this is interpreted by the Explorer system to mean 2000, and not just zeros.

First, set the date forward to May 14 2000. Then use an editor – Notepad is handy for this – to create a file 'datetest.txt'. Verify that the datestamp is indeed 14/05/00. Now use the Explorer to search for the file within the date range December 1 1999 – July 1 2000.

Start the Explorer and initiate a file search:

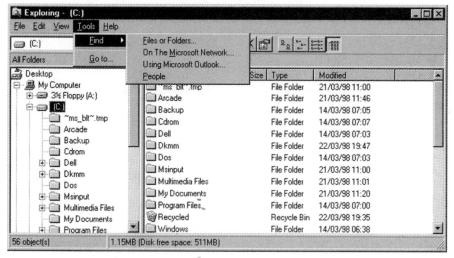

Then search for the file 'datetest.txt':

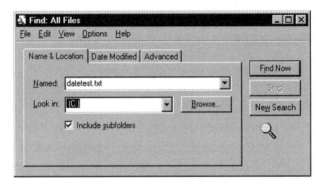

Specify a date-range for the search, and select 'Find Now':

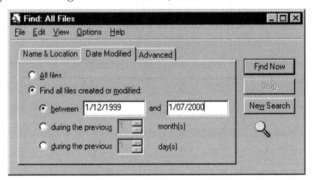

If Explorer successfully finds the file, the result is displayed as follows:

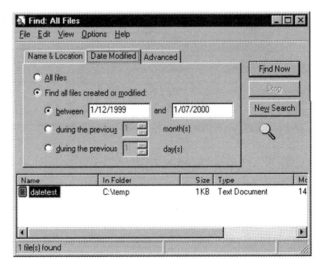

This confirms that the operating system and its utilities, on this PC at least, can handle files with 2000 and later dates. If the file's datestamp were written wrongly to the filesystem, programs using that file might fail. Even if the datestamp is correct, of course, applications using the file might still fail on post-1999 dates read from the file's data. That is the 'application' as opposed to the 'system' side of the problem and is covered as such in Chapter 5.

Upgrading a PC operating system

Consideration of applying the Y2K fix to PCs is often limited to the system-clock and filesystem topics dealt with above. But, in the real world, the problem is much more difficult than that: at least for obsolete operating environments such as Windows 3.x, it is not enough to upgrade the BIOS or tamper with dates. The operating system itself as a computer program is not Y2K-compliant and needs to be upgraded. This is also the case with earlier versions of Windows 95 and OS/2. Many organisations are using the Y2K-enforced update of their PC asset bases as a catalyst for a more general update and streamlining of the software on those PCs.

There are two ways of upgrading a PC operating system: upgrading it or replacing it. Anyone with experience of the process will recommend the latter. The question then arises of how to replace a client operating system while retaining some at least of the configuration settings it holds, as well as application data generated in the period since it was installed. Compounding the problem is the need to perform the replacement procedure for a large number of PCs which may not all be starting from the same 'base'. Some may be running Windows 3.x, some OS/2, and so on.

The first purpose of this book is to examine the direct impact of the Year 2000 problem, not to get into all the details of operating system upgrade on large numbers of PCs. In any case, system software installation is a large field of expertise in its own right and full coverage of it is beyond the scope of a book of this size. All that I do here is give a general presentation of the issues involved and the steps that you will have to consider in updating your organisation's PCs as part of the Y2K repair project.

The process of upgrading operating systems, including their network software components, is one fraught with 'Catch-22'-type situations. These include:

- How to start the PC running ('boot up') when its hard disk may be blank, unformatted or just not contain an operating system. Such a PC is referred to hereafter as a 'blank' PC.

- How to make a 'blank' PC execute network software so that it can 'talk to' the rest of the world.

- How to install an operating system and its network software, probably over a network to the (blank!) PC, with little or no user intervention ('unattended install') while still configuring it with network address, user ID and other information.

IS departments responsible for the maintenance of distributed client/server environments spend a major proportion of their time overcoming these difficulties and defining procedures to work around them. In addressing the Year 2000 repair of client systems, the Y2K project team must also deal with these problems.

Boot sequence

Operating systems are usually resident on a 'system disk' (typically the C: drive on PCs) and the computer 'boots from' that disk. The boot process involves starting the PC from a small set of instructions stored at a known location on the disk – the Master Boot Record in Windows 95/98 – followed by the execution of a minimal copy of the operating system in memory. This then reads from disk ('boots', as in pulling oneself up 'by the bootstraps') the operating system programs proper. These execute, and bring the computer and all its operations under their control. Any program that runs subsequently does so under the control of the executing operating system.

In order to install an operating system and network software to a blank PC, the PC must first be 'booted' from a diskette or some medium other than the PC's system disk. If the medium is a diskette, as it usually is, it is called a 'boot diskette'. The boot diskette has the following characteristics:

- A boot record – when the diskette is in the PC's diskette drive and the computer is started, the PC will automatically boot from the diskette.

- A minimal operating system – in Windows implementations, this is COMMAND.COM.

- Minimal network software – device drivers and configuration files – to allow the PC to communicate with outside systems while running from the diskette only.

- A 'script' – a program on the diskette which partitions and formats the system disk and transfers the operating system proper from the location where its 'image' is stored.

The Y2K project team has determined that some of the organisation's client PCs must be re-initialised with a new operating system and network software. Regardless of which exact procedure is used to effect this upgrade, a boot diskette – or equivalent medium – will always be used.

Installation strategies

There are three ways in which an operating system and network software can be installed to a blank PC:

- A technician visits the PC and installs the operating system software on the PC from a diskette and CD-ROM. After this, the technician must configure the PC with network-address, user ID and other information.

- An unattended installation: an automated equivalent of the above. The operating system installation files are stored on a network server or other accessible medium. Pre-prepared 'answer files' are used to supply the answers during the installation that would otherwise be given by the technician.

- Installation from an 'image': the operating system is pre-installed to an accessible drive, probably on a network server. Included in the installation may be application programs and any other files that, along with the operating system collectively constitute the organisation's standard gold build.

The first of these alternatives is impractical for all but small network environments. The installation from CD and subsequent software configuration will take anything from 30 minutes to several hours, per PC being installed. If your organisation has hundreds or thousands of PCs, – in fact, more than about 50 – a more efficient way must be found.

The unattended install is a feature of the Windows NT/2000 configuration tools. It can arrange for the installation of the operating system and applications to client PCs over the network from installation media stored on CD or another accessible location. To start the procedure, the PC is booted from a diskette, from which a minimal operating system is run. Minimal network communications are established with a network server. Pre-programmed answer files are then used to supply all the responses required, automating the conventional installation of the operating system from the network server. Unattended install works well with Windows NT/2000. However, not all PC operating systems have an equivalent and there is a lot of detail and time-consuming effort involved in setting it up.

Gold build

The third possibility is to load, to each client PC which is to be upgraded, an 'image' containing the already-installed operating system, the network software and any required application software also already-installed to the image. Once set up, the gold build and its install procedures offer the fastest and most reliable means of upgrading client PCs on a large scale with Y2K-compliant operating system and application software.

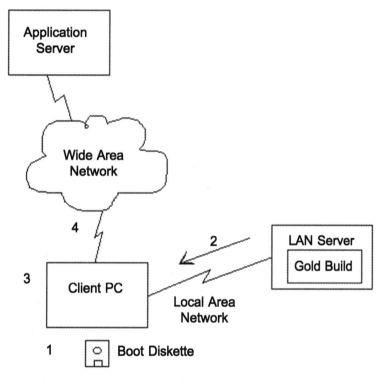

Figure 4.1 The gold build approach

As always, the PC to be upgraded is booted from a special boot diskette (1). This starts the minimal operating system, starts communication with the network server, partitions and formats the PC's system disk and copies the 'image' over the network (2) from the network server to the disk. Rebooting the PC from the system disk (3) should result in an operational client, running with all the required Y2K software in place and with network links to the application server established (4).

If you think all this sounds too easy, your suspicions are well-founded.

Firstly, I have deliberately glossed over a lot of detail:

- Creating a bootable diskette is easy, but what files constitute the minimal operating system? They are (in the Windows environment) COMMAND.COM, IO.SYS and CONFIG.SYS.

- What is the 'minimal network software'? This is the set of files needed to allow the PC to 'see' the gold build on the LAN server. Different sets of files are needed depending on whether this is a NetWare, NT or other server.

- How exactly is the PC's disk partitioned and the boot record created? This will depend on the type of disk unit in the PC.

- What about the increased network traffic load imposed by deployment over the network to hundreds or thousands of PCs of system images of anywhere between 20MB and 200MB in size? Careful scheduling of deployment is needed here if business use of the network's bandwidth is not to be affected.

Then come the difficulties, mostly related to unique characteristics of the PC and specific information required for that PC, especially network address and user ID. The main problems are these:

- In order that it can start communication with the LAN server, a unique boot diskette will be required for every type of PC network card used in your organisation. This is fine if they are all the same but, in most organisations several different types are to be found. With several different boot diskettes in existence, care is needed to ensure that each PC has one of the right type.

- A similar hardware dependency arises for every variation on disk unit used in the organisation's PCs. Potentially, every different type will have to be partitioned and formatted differently, again multiplying the number of boot-diskette variations that must be maintained.

- Suppose that TCP/IP is used as the WAN network protocol. How does the client PC get its unique IP address in order to establish the link at (4) with the application server?

- Similarly, how does the client PC get its unique user ID information – 'profile' information under the newer versions of Windows?

The simplest solution to the first two questions is to have as few hardware variations possible in your organisation's stock of PCs. The more variations there are, the more the number of boot diskettes will multiply. In fact, many businesses, large and small, enforce a policy of standardised PC specifications exactly for this reason.

The questions of information unique to each PC are difficult. When being initialised, the (blank) PC cannot know the user-specific information or its IP address. Except for these, the boot-diskette-initiated PC upgrade is entirely without user intervention: the PC boots from the diskette and 15 or 20 minutes later, it has been initialised with the gold-build operating system, network software and applications. All these items, thanks to prior planning, are Y2K-compliant. Now we are asking a technically-unqualified user to intervene and actually input some data in response to prompts presented during the boot-up procedure.

This is allowable with the user ID; the user should know his or her own name, or the PC asset-tag number, whichever is being used. The user cannot, however, be expected to know and enter an IP address in response to a prompt; this is a job for a qualified technician. Depending on its configuration, we could probably get the IP address from the application server – if the PC had the network link to that system for which the IP address is required in the first place. It is this Catch-22 that we must escape. There are at least three ways of doing so:

- Implement DHCP (Dynamic Host Control Protocol) on the LAN server. This automatically assigns an IP address to the PC when it boots up with its newly-loaded gold-build operating system, and allows the PC to communicate with the application server.

- If DHCP is not being used, maintain a table (User/PC ID by IP address) on the boot diskette, which can be searched for IP address when the user inputs his or her ID. This approach has the weakness that the table – which must be on every boot diskette – must be kept up to date. If it is not, assignments of IP addresses to PCs will be wrong, with consequent network address clashes. An improvement is to store a single copy of the table on the LAN server.

- 'Lift' the IP address from the previous operating system in place on the PC, if any. This is done from the same 'script' on the diskette which downloads the gold build – but before the original contents of the system disk have been erased by formatting. A problem with this approach is that it fails where there was no previous operating system on the PC, and that finding the IP address will be a different procedure for each operating system variant.

In practice, if DHCP is not configured, the second approach – with IP table on the LAN server – is used. The third option – lifting the IP address – raises the related question of how to carry forward to the upgraded PC user data and preference files that may have existed on the original non-Y2K-compliant client. The only realistic answer to this is that the user should have a backup of that data, to be restored to the upgraded system when it has been installed.

Large-scale upgrade of PCs, along with all the techniques and details involved, is an extremely complex subject. Many excellent systems management specialists spend their working lives doing little else. It is just not realistic to pretend that the Y2K problem can be addressed only in terms of fixing application software on the mainframe or server. The larger job, in fact, may lie in fixing all those client PCs. While not detailed, the outline given in this chapter should serve as a template which you, or your organisation's technical staff, can use to investigate the matter further.

4.4 Network and server

This section considers possible non-Y2K-compliance in network software (the software 'stack' to be found on every system connected to the network), LAN servers, and the application server systems that run the 'back-end' database and other applications on which enquiries are made across the network by the clients.

Compared with the number of clients, there are very few LAN servers and even fewer back-end application servers. Fixing them for Y2K is not associated with the same problems of scalability that must be addressed in the case of client PCs. Remember that, in this chapter, we are concerned with the 'infrastructure'; applying Y2K repairs to the application software concentrated on application servers is covered in Chapter 5.

Network software – the 'stack' – is almost always nowadays an integral part of the operating system on the computer to be connected to the network. As such, if the operating system itself is Y2K-compliant, the network software is likely to be also. At worst, it will be necessary to source from the supplier of the operating system a patch or service pack that will Y2K-fix the network software. In principle, it is best for all computers on your organisation's network to upgrade the operating system – including network software – to a level certified by its originator as Y2K-compliant.

LAN server

If the operating system controlling the computer that acts as a LAN server is not Y2K compliant, this fact will manifest in the ways we have already seen for client PCs. The system clock on the LAN server will not store dates later than December 31 1999. Files written to the filesystem on the LAN server may have wrong datestamps if they are written later than that date.

LAN server operating systems include OS/2, Windows NT/2000, Novell NetWare and many variants of UNIX. The latest version of

OS/2 – Version 4 – is Y2K-clean but earlier versions are not. The same is the case with Windows NT/2000 and NetWare 4.x. UNIX, as ever, is a special case.

UNIX calculates all its times in seconds from the start of January 1 1970. It uses a long integer (32 bits) to do so and can increment from zero up to 2,147,483,647 seconds. There are 31,556,926 seconds in a solar year. The UNIX timing scheme is good for a little over 68 years: we encounter a Y2K-like problem early in 2038. UNIX is therefore Y2K-clean, with any problem deferred a further 38 years. Incidentally, nothing in the UNIX implementation 'hard-wires' the 2038 date: the limitation is imposed only by the current 32-bit size of the C language long integer. As soon as that is increased, presumably to 64 bits, on all UNIX systems, the problem disappears.

Trivia: a 64-bit long integer date is good for 584,554,530,500 years from now – about 127 times the estimated age of the Earth so far!

The effect of Y2K dependencies in LAN server operating systems is more pervasive than it is with client PCs. As its name implies, a LAN server 'serves' a number of client PCs – usually several hundred. Those PCs may take their system dates from the LAN server and will receive data files from the server. Even if a client PC has been Y2K-repaired, then, it may get a wrong system date or wrongly-datestamped files from its LAN server. This will have all the bad effects on the client's operation that we have already seen. It is possible also that the LAN server runs applications that will exchange files with other systems on the network. If this is the case, those applications must also be checked for internal Y2K-compliance using the techniques outlined in Chapter 5.

From an 'infrastructure' viewpoint, applying the Y2K fix to a LAN server is a matter of upgrading its network operating system to a Y2K-compliant level. This should be done first – before all the client PCs that it serves. Because they are relatively few in number, it is possible for a technician to visit each server for the purpose of making the upgrade. The upgrade must be carefully timed in order not to impact on the networked clients. In addition, all shared data files must be backed up before the upgrade and restored afterwards.

Application server

Ensuring that the application server system software is Y2K-compliant is usually straightforward. In the first place, there will be one or a handful of servers, so scalability is not a problem. The operating system will be well-known – usually an IBM mainframe operating system such as MVS, Digital Equipment's OpenVMS or a variant of UNIX such as Solaris (Sun Microsystems), HP-UX (Hewlett Packard) or AIX (IBM). Since the server is a large and expensive system, the supplier is able reliably to certify the state of Year 2000 readiness of the resident operating system. The most likely problems to be encountered are:

- The operating system is an obsolete non-Y2K-clean, variant.

- A mainframe server is an obsolete version, lacking certain hardware needed to support a Y2K-clean operating system.

Both these circumstances are most likely to come about in mainframe environments. Many organisations using mainframes as servers deliberately operate 'back-rev' (not the latest model) operating systems in order not to be the first to encounter software problems. A surprising number acquired an operating system such as DOS/VSE (an early 370-architecture IBM operating system) in, say, 1975 and never upgraded. In order to be Y2K-compliant, both the 'back-rev' MVS and obsolete DOS/VSE systems must be upgraded to a level recommended by IBM. The latter, however, will be a major migration, requiring new hardware, software utilities and file conversions.

Operating systems are not the only mainframe server software that the Y2K project team must be concerned with. System software, including COBOL and other compilers, database systems such as DB2 and IMS, and CICS transaction processing software must be identified and evaluated. Many users of mainframe and IBM 'mid-range' AS/400 computers will find they are also on 'back-rev' versions of some or all of these software systems. Just because a mainframe COBOL program, for example, has been made Y2K-compliant in its source code, screen displays and the data files that it uses, it does not necessarily mean that all is well. If an obsolete compiler and linkage editor are used to compile the program and produce a load module, the executable program may contain non-Y2K-compliant run-time modules and will fail. Several products exist – an example is the Edge Portfolio Analyzer – for use in the mainframe environment that assess load modules, identify the level of compiler used to create them and provide summaries of their attributes as well as the facilities they use.

Analysis of the system software environment on a mainframe server will involve your organisation, in co-operation with the system supplier (often IBM), in using tools to determine the revision levels of the operating system and other software products being used. After establishing what is on the system, it is then a matter of upgrading, if necessary, to the software revision levels specified by IBM.

Any upgrade to a server – not just a mainframe – must be a carefully-planned event. Business disruption must be minimised, which may involve using a backup production system while the system software migration is achieved. Backups of data files, which are part of the culture in mainframe and 'mission-critical' server environments, are, of course, vital.

5 | Fixing applications

5.1 Introduction

In contrast to Chapter 4, this chapter looks at the Year 2000 problem from a server and application-programming standpoint. At the start of Chapter 1, there is a concise statement of the problem. A given year represented in two digits may wrongly be assumed by an application program to be of the 20th century; also, the year '00' may wrongly be assumed by an application not to be a leap year. If an application program makes either of these assumptions, it is likely to fail in execution or to give wrong results.

Most legacy business software in fact makes these assumptions – containing what I have called date-dependencies – and will fail after December 31 1999 (before, in some cases) if nothing is done. This chapter concentrates on demonstrating and evaluating the various programming techniques used to overcome these dependencies and make the applications 'Y2K-compliant'.

Which technique to use depends on the nature of a specific date-dependency as it is encountered in application software. Recall from Chapter 3 the classification of date-dependencies. They are, in decreasing order of seriousness:

- Class 1 dates: dates which span more than 100 years but in which the year is represented by only two year-digits and which are processed by code sensitive to the current date. For these dates, file formats and data representations must be changed to show four-digit years explicitly.

- Class 2 dates: dates referring to events a short distance in the past or future which imply the century they are part of. These dates can be fixed for Y2K in program logic only; file formats and data representations need not be changed.

- Class 3 dates: dates which are Year 2000-ready from the outset and for which no modification need be made to the application or its files.

Class 1 dates are those which need to be converted from two-digit-year format to four-digit-year (century) format, where they occur in files used by applications. Such dates stored in files need to be *expanded*. Where files are expanded from 'YY' format to 'CCYY' format, all programs that use those files must be adjusted to 'map' to the new definition. That adjustment is one aspect of the 'Y2K repair'. Date expansion in certain cases is unavoidable and, because of its knock-on effect on other programs, it is the most 'expensive' kind of Y2K-related code and data change. In this chapter, I focus on how to minimise the extent of date expansion required in any Y2K project.

Date expansion is required for Class 1 dates. However, only a small proportion of dates used in typical application files are Class 1. Many dates are stored with two-digit years but their meaning is clear from the context in which they are used. For example, if a life-assurance term ends, according to the documentation in the year 18, it is almost certain that that means 2018 and not 1918. In cases like this, date expansion is unnecessary; all that is needed is a technique known as *date windowing*, by which the 18 is interpreted to mean 2018 but 95 means 1995. To perform date expansion on a date field that only needs date windowing is very wasteful, both in terms of the extra programming that must be done to implement expansion *and* in the proportionate amount of extra testing needed.

For Class 3 dates, no work is needed at all. Such dates include those already having 4-digit years; unused date fields; and dates which are read by one or more applications but are never used in calculations or tests. It is even more wasteful to Y2K-convert these. The assessment phase of the Y2K project (see Chapter 3) should identify all Class 3 dates and eliminate them from further consideration.

Programming techniques

This chapter enumerates the main techniques used in fixing date-dependencies. The two most common – date expansion and date windowing – are given first. I also give some advantages and disadvantages of each approach. Each technique is both described in narrative and then implemented in a sample COBOL program.

Most of the world's business applications are written in COBOL, so it seems reasonable that solutions to Y2K date-dependencies should be expressed in that language. Many Y2K books avoid a level of detail that involves actual programming. However, many readers of a book such as this will have some familiarity with COBOL or, at least, some programming knowledge. In Chapter 4, I present some of the issues surrounding BIOS compatibility for Y2K, and the difficulties of upgrading client PCs over the network. Similarly, on the programming side, it is of more practical value to the reader that this book should express the fixes as real programs than adopt the kind of narrative compromise common to most publications about Y2K. If you do not know COBOL, be assured that it is not a difficult language and that I highlight the essential points in the examples that follow. Also, all the programs are based on the same simplified payroll-system model which you should find reasonably intuitive.

Problem COBOL code

The Y2K dates problem, as expressed in COBOL, is this. A date quantity is represented in memory or on file according to one of the following data definitions:

```
01  OLD-GREG-DATE.
      02    OLD-GREG-YY PIC 99.
      02    OLD-GREG-MM PIC 99.
      02    OLD-GREG-DD PIC 99.

01  OLD-JUL-DATE.
      02    OLD-JUL-YY  PIC 99.
      02    OLD-JUL-DDD PIC 999.
```

Using OLD-GREG-DATE, in a program, for example, refers to the entire year-month-day entity. OLD-GREG-YY, by comparison, refers only to the year component of the date. Because the year-fields in both definitions are two-digit fields, both these definitions assume the year to be in the range 00 to 99 and, implicitly, that we are dealing with the twentieth century.

Finding the problem code

As part of the Y2K project, the affected code must firstly be found (inventoried) and assessed. The next step is to fix the code. Finding the code is by no means as easy as it sounds. For example, the data-item names may not be as intuitive and sensible as those above. A year number might be stored in a data item called WS-ODDSNENDS and might be quite difficult to identify. Hard-coded checks may be done in a program against numbers such as 75 or 99 but you may not be able to tell just from looking at them if they are processing dates or not. Not every division by 4 is a leap-year check. Not every test for a variable being in the range 1 to 12 is a test for a valid month number. How do you know whether or not a key (used to search an indexed file) contains a two-digit date specification? No program or software tool has yet been devised that can find *all* Y2K dependencies. Inspection by real, human, COBOL programmers is more than ever necessary.

That said, the range of available tools is extensive and useful. One of the early tasks of the Y2K project is identification and selection of appropriate software tools. Tools are needed for BIOS testing, PC and mainframe inventory, source-code search, load-module (on mainframes) analysis, and general testing. Hundreds of these are available from a large choice of suppliers.

Your organisation may co-operate with a supplier such as IBM, MicroFocus or Computer Associates – to name a very few – in identifying which Y2K software tools it will use. If you have not yet identified any and want to know where to start, the best place is on the Internet. The main problem on the Web is that there is too much Y2K-related information to assimilate. For example, if you use a Web browser to search globally on the string: 'Year 2000 Tools' a list of about 900 matching entries appears. It is difficult to know where to start – and this is only one search. Many more Y2K-related Web sites will be uncovered with different searches. I recommend two sites in particular. The first is the Year 2000 Tools and Services Catalog maintained by Mitre Corp., at this Web site:

www.mitre.org/research/y2k

The site is jointly maintained by the US Department of Defense and the Electronic Systems Center, and is as near to a comprehensive listing of Y2K-related software products and services as I have encountered. It features the offerings of a large number of suppliers in many categories. Enter the Tools and Services Catalog (Figure 5.1) then search on 'Platform-specific tools'. You will find a most useful matrix of Y2K software tools arranged by system type and purpose (Figure 5.2). The numeric columns respectively refer to mainframes, workstations and PCs and provide links to the indicated numbers of software tools in the categories shown in the leftmost column.

Another very useful Web site is IBM's own, at the address:

www.ibm.com/IBM/year2000

This site (Figure 5.3) is of remarkable depth. It provides, among other information, a matrix of all IBM's Y2K software tools, listed by Y2K functional category and IBM computer and operating system. A small part of that matrix is shown in Figure 5.4.

Using the Mitre and IBM sites, you should check the tools supplied by IBM, MicroFocus, Viasoft, Computer Associates, Isogon Corp., Platinum Inc. and others. I have always liked MicroFocus utilities: for Year 2000, the company's SoftFactory 2000 suite of tools applies to both the mainframe and PC sides of the client/server divide.

But this is just a personal opinion; search for yourself, if you have access to the Web. If you do not have access, get it; it is amazing how much free information can be found on the Web when searching

5.1 Introduction

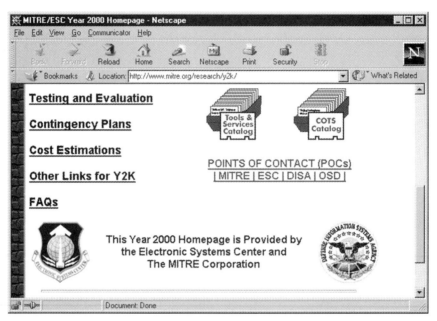

Figure 5.1 The Tools and Services Catalog at the Mitre Corp site.

	MAINFRAMES	WORKSTATIONS	PCs
Inventory	10	5	13
Assessment*	23	21	16
Repair*	23	28	33
Test Generation*	10	14	13
Test Analysis*	9	9	7
Simulators	9	5	3
Configuration Management	4	7	3
Project Management*	7	9	7

Figure 5.2 Mitre's listing of shareware tools arranged by system type.

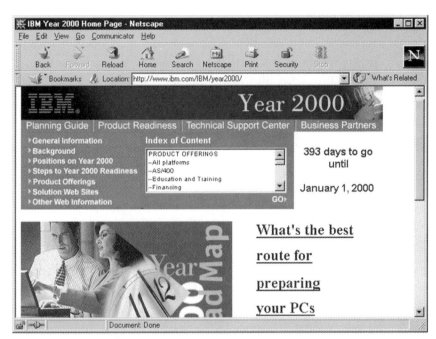

Figure 5.3 The Year 2000 Home Page at IBM's Web site.

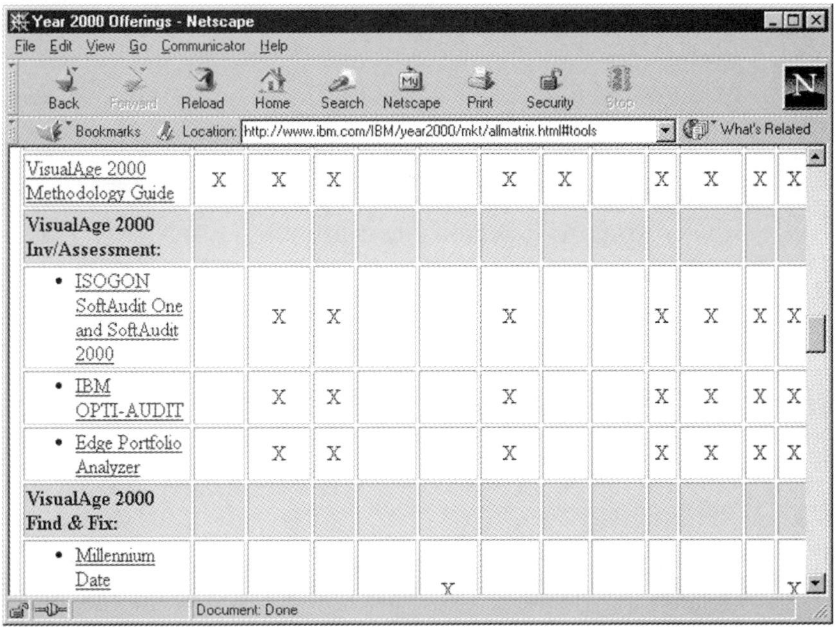

Figure 5.4 IBM's Y2K software tools, listed by functional category.

for specific information. Many of these sites also provide free software, including BIOS check-and-fix modules. There is no point in my trying to list further tools here. There are just too many for that to be useful, although Chapter 7 suggests some further, mostly UK-based, information sources.

5.2 Date expansion

I have already pointed out that there are two main approaches to the Y2K fix: convert files and code; and, alternatively, use a scheme of 'windowing'. The remainder of this section looks at the process of conversion.

The most obvious solution to the Y2K problem as it affects COBOL programs is to expand data files to 4-digit year representation and modify code accordingly. It sounds easy and, in fact, it is easy, but it is always a major change to files and code. It is, in effect, treating all dates as Class 1 dates which, as we have seen, is unnecessary. This section shows how to deal with Class 1 dates, but the windowing techniques shown in the sections following should be used for Class 2 dates. Major change implies errors and extensive testing for elimination of errors – a time-consuming process.

Here, to illustrate the conversion process, is a COBOL program that maintains a payroll file called SEQPMAST.DAT. This file is a collection of data records, actually appearing on disk like this:

```
Conor Sexton         1234    C10029M     Rathfarnham, Dublin,
Ireland. 9511090100000000000000Bubble Car        Mike Cash
2345       S25039M        Jordan  Hill,  Oxford,  UK.
8712120500000000500000Ferrari Testarossa Rebecca Hammersley
5643       S10023F        Summertown,  Oxford,  UK.
9601010250000000250000E-type  Jag            Neil Fawcet
0089       S29045M        Blenheim,  Oxford,  UK.
8504010900000000100000Mercedes  S600
```

Most of the details are not important: the file holds a lot of payroll-related information. There are four records in the file, one each in the name of a person. In the first record, the date associated with my name is 951109. This is intended to be November 9, 1995 but it is, of course, ambiguous in the Y2K context. Each of the other records also contains a two-digit-year date. By our earlier definition, if it is uncertain whether 95 means 1995 or 2095, these are Class 1 dates and require date expansion.

The solution is to write a COBOL program that will convert this file (actually convert while copying to a new file) to the four-digit-year format. The program is called DATECONV.CBL. Here it is:

```
***********************************************************************
*                                                                     *
*                      DATECONV.CBL                                    *
*                                                                      *
*  This program reads the payroll master file and converts date       *
*  information stored there. File organization is sequential.          *
*                                                                      *
***********************************************************************
 IDENTIFICATION DIVISION.
 PROGRAM-ID. DATECONV.

 ENVIRONMENT DIVISION.

 INPUT-OUTPUT SECTION.
 FILE-CONTROL.
     SELECT OPTIONAL I-PAYROLL-MASTER
     ASSIGN TO "SEQPMAST.DAT"
     ORGANIZATION IS SEQUENTIAL
     ACCESS MODE IS SEQUENTIAL
     FILE STATUS IS WS-I-PR-STATUS.

     SELECT OPTIONAL O-PAYROLL-CONV
     ASSIGN TO "SEQPCONV.DAT"
     ORGANIZATION IS SEQUENTIAL
     ACCESS MODE IS SEQUENTIAL
     FILE STATUS IS WS-O-CONV-STATUS.

 DATA DIVISION.
 FILE SECTION.
 FD  I-PAYROLL-MASTER
     BLOCK CONTAINS 20 RECORDS
     LABEL RECORDS ARE STANDARD
     RECORD CONTAINS 111 CHARACTERS.
     01  I-PR-RECORD.
           02 FILLER  PIC X(111).
```

```
FD  O-PAYROLL-CONV
    BLOCK CONTAINS 20 RECORDS
    LABEL RECORDS ARE STANDARD
    RECORD CONTAINS 119 CHARACTERS.
01  O-PR-RECORD.
        02 FILLER      PIC X(119).

WORKING-STORAGE SECTION.
01  WS-PR-RECORD.
    02 WS-PR-NAME      PIC X(20).
    02 WS-PR-EMPNO       PIC X(8).
    02 WS-PR-EMPTYPE     PIC X.
    02 WS-PR-GRADE       PIC 99.
    02 WS-PR-AGE       PIC 999.
    02 WS-PR-GENDER      PIC X.
    02 WS-PR-REFNO       PIC 9999.
    02 WS-PR-ADDR      PIC X(30).
    02 WS-PR-EMPDATE.
        03 WS-PR-YY      PIC 99.
        03 WS-PR-MM      PIC 99.
        03 WS-PR-DD      PIC 99.
    02 WS-PR-PAY       PIC 9(6)V99.
    02 WS-PR-BONUS       PIC 9(6)V99.
    02 WS-PR-CAR       PIC X(20).

01  WS-CV-RECORD.
    02 WS-PR-NAME      PIC X(20).
    02 WS-PR-EMPNO       PIC X(8).
    02 WS-PR-EMPTYPE     PIC X.
    02 WS-PR-GRADE       PIC 99.
    02 WS-PR-AGE       PIC 999.
    02 WS-PR-GENDER      PIC X.
    02 WS-PR-REFNO       PIC 9999.
    02 WS-PR-ADDR      PIC X(30).
    02 WS-PR-EMPDATE.
        03 WS-PR-YY      PIC 99.
        03 WS-PR-MM      PIC 99.
        03 WS-PR-DD      PIC 99.
    02 WS-PR-PAY       PIC 9(6)V99.
    02 WS-PR-BONUS       PIC 9(6)V99.
    02 WS-PR-CAR       PIC X(20).
    02 WS-CV-EMPDATE.
        03 WS-CV-CC      PIC 99.
        03 WS-PR-YY      PIC 99.
        03 WS-PR-MM      PIC 99.
        03 WS-PR-DD      PIC 99.
```

```
    01  WS-I-END-FILE    PIC X VALUE "N".
    01  WS-I-PR-STATUS    PIC XX.
    01  WS-O-CONV-STATUS    PIC XX.

PROCEDURE DIVISION.
A-MAIN-LINE SECTION.
A-000-MAIN.
    PERFORM AA-INITIALISE.
    READ I-PAYROLL-MASTER AT END
        MOVE "Y" TO WS-I-END-FILE.
    PERFORM AB-PROCESS UNTIL WS-I-END-FILE = "Y".
    PERFORM AC-TERMINATE.

A-999-EXIT.
    STOP RUN.

AA-INITIALISE SECTION.
AA-000-OPEN.
    OPEN INPUT I-PAYROLL-MASTER.
    IF WS-I-PR-STATUS NOT EQUAL ZERO THEN
        DISPLAY "Error " WS-I-PR-STATUS
            " opening employee master file."
        GO TO A-999-EXIT
    END-IF.

    OPEN OUTPUT O-PAYROLL-CONV.
    IF WS-O-CONV-STATUS NOT EQUAL ZERO THEN
        DISPLAY "Error " WS-O-CONV-STATUS
            " opening converted-date file."
        GO TO A-999-EXIT
    END-IF.

AA-999-EXIT.
    EXIT.

AB-PROCESS SECTION.
AB-000-CONVERT-DATA.
    MOVE I-PR-RECORD TO WS-PR-RECORD.
    MOVE ZEROS TO WS-PR-REFNO OF WS-PR-RECORD.
    MOVE CORRESPONDING WS-PR-RECORD TO WS-CV-RECORD.
    MOVE CORRESPONDING WS-PR-EMPDATE OF WS-PR-RECORD
        TO WS-CV-EMPDATE.
    MOVE 19 TO WS-CV-CC.

AB-010-WRITE-CONVERTED.
    MOVE WS-CV-RECORD TO O-PR-RECORD.
    DISPLAY O-PR-RECORD.
    WRITE O-PR-RECORD.
```

```
    IF WS-O-CONV-STATUS NOT EQUAL ZERO THEN
        DISPLAY "Error " WS-O-CONV-STATUS
              " writing converted-date file."
          GO TO A-999-EXIT
    END-IF.

AB-020-READ-DATA.
    READ I-PAYROLL-MASTER AT END
    MOVE "Y" TO WS-I-END-FILE.

AB-999-EXIT.
    EXIT.

AC-TERMINATE SECTION.
AC-000-CLOSE.
    CLOSE  I-PAYROLL-MASTER.
    CLOSE  O-PAYROLL-CONV.

AC-999-EXIT.
    EXIT.
```

Do not be intimidated by this program; it is actually very straightforward. In essence, it reads all the records from the input payroll master file, SEQPMAST.DAT, and writes them in turn to the output (date-expanded) file SEQPCONV.DAT. Note that the SEQPMAST.DAT input record I-PR-RECORD is of length 111, while the SEQPCONV.DAT output record O-PR-RECORD is 119 characters long. The difference is the eight characters required to accommodate an eight-character CCYYMMDD-format date in the expanded output record.

Holding areas for the input and output records are defined in WORKING-STORAGE. The group data item names of these areas are WS-PR-RECORD (input) and WS-CV-RECORD (output).

The program DATECONV.CBL reads all the records from the input file in sequence and writes them all in sequence to the output (converted) file. The critical code that effects the conversion is this:

```
AB-000-CONVERT-DATA.
    MOVE I-PR-RECORD TO WS-PR-RECORD.
    MOVE ZEROS TO WS-PR-REFNO OF WS-PR-RECORD.
    MOVE CORRESPONDING WS-PR-RECORD TO WS-CV-RECORD.
    MOVE CORRESPONDING WS-PR-EMPDATE OF WS-PR-RECORD
```

```
                TO WS-CV-EMPDATE.
    MOVE 19 TO WS-CV-CC.
```

The first statement in the paragraph moves the input record to its holding area. The first MOVE CORRESPONDING assigns the subordinate data items of WS-PR-RECORD to subordinate data items of the same names in WS-CV-RECORD. The expanded date WS-CV-EMPDATE is new to WS-CV-RECORD – it has no counterpart in the input record – so the first MOVE CORRESPONDING has no effect on it. The two dates are subject of a separate MOVE CORRESPONDING, which assigns the three parts of the six-digit date from the input file to WS-CV-EMPDATE in the output holding area. The two digits '19' are then moved to the CENTURY field in WS-CV-EMPDATE. From this the output-file record is written, and we end up with an expanded file.

The contents of the output file, SEQPCONV.DAT, are these:

```
Conor Sexton         1234    C10029M0000Rathfarnham, Dublin,
Ireland. 9511090100000000000000Bubble Car          19951109Mike
Cash            2345     S25039M0000Jordan Hill, Oxford, UK.
8712120500000000500000Ferrari Testarossa    19871212Rebecca
Hammersley   5643      S10023F0000Summertown, Oxford, UK.
9601010250000000250000E-type Jag            19960101Neil
Fawcet          0089     S29045M0000Blenheim, Oxford, UK.
8504010900000001000000Mercedes S600         19850401
```

You can see that the original dates remain the same, but that four-digit-year dates have been added to the end of each record. '19' is arbitrarily assigned on the assumption that all existing dates in the file would be from the 20th century. This might not be the case – consider as an example the expiry date of a 20-year life-assurance policy – so, in converting files, you will have to know for the application in question whether to use '19' or '20'.

The apparent duplication of dates – the short version is retained and the Y2K version added – is deliberate. It means that existing, pre-Y2K programs may still be able to work with the expanded file or, at most, that only a simple 'bridge' program will be need to convert the file back to its original, non-expanded, state. This practice of adding the whole 8-digit date at the end of the record is a very important technique for efficiency.

The process of date expansion is reasonably straightforward, although on *huge* files, it can take time and lots of disk space. The difficulty is that all COBOL code that subsequently handles the converted file must change its logic to accommodate the newly-four-digit year. This is a task for your organisation's chosen date-dependency search tool, but some manual checking and fixing will be needed to make sure that all dependencies have been caught.

5.3 Sliding windows

Files containing Class 1 dates must be converted. For Class 2 dates, conversion is unnecessary and wasteful. The technique needed is one of 'windowing' the date – defining a 100-year period, within which applications are assumed to operate. The most common form of windowing is the technique known as sliding windows. Dates stored on file in the pre-Y2K YYMMDD format are not expanded. Instead, the two-digit year is assumed to be in a range based on a displacement from the current year. The current year is found from the system date.

We adopt a business rule that specifies a year 'horizon', say 2038. which is an arbitrary 40-year displacement ahead of the current system date. Then, applications using files containing non-expanded dates treat all those dates as being in the range 1939 to 2038. If the two-digit year value is 85, applications assume the year to be 1985; if the value is 17, the date is assumed to be 2017. Notice that, because the base year for calculating the displacement is derived from the system date, the period of the window moves. The sliding window technique may therefore constitute a *permanent* solution, at a huge saving in effort compared to file- and date-expansion.

Here is a program, very similar to DATECONV.CBL and using the same payroll model, which applies the sliding window technique to the six-digit date stored in the payroll master file SEQPMAST.DAT. Unlike in DATECONV.CBL, there is no output file: the date in the payroll master is *treated as read-only* and the century to which it belongs is *interpreted in the program's logic.* The program, DATESWIN.CBL does not write to an output file, but it does display on screen its interpretation of the dates. Here is the program:

```
**********************************************************************
*                                                                    *
*                        DATESWIN.CBL                                *
*                                                                    *
*  This program reads the payroll master file and filters date       *
*  information using a sliding window. File organization is          *
*  sequential.                                                        *
*                                                                    *
**********************************************************************

 IDENTIFICATION DIVISION.
 PROGRAM-ID. DATESWIN.

 ENVIRONMENT DIVISION.

 INPUT-OUTPUT SECTION.
 FILE-CONTROL.
     SELECT OPTIONAL I-PAYROLL-MASTER
     ASSIGN TO "SEQPMAST.DAT"
     ORGANIZATION IS SEQUENTIAL
     ACCESS MODE IS SEQUENTIAL
     FILE STATUS IS WS-I-PR-STATUS.

 DATA DIVISION.
 FILE SECTION.
 FD  I-PAYROLL-MASTER
     BLOCK CONTAINS 20 RECORDS
     LABEL RECORDS ARE STANDARD
     RECORD CONTAINS 111 CHARACTERS.
 01  I-PR-RECORD.
     02 FILLER           PIC X(111).

 WORKING-STORAGE SECTION.
 01  WS-PR-RECORD.
     02 WS-PR-NAME       PIC X(20).
     02 WS-PR-EMPNO      PIC X(8).
     02 WS-PR-EMPTYPE    PIC X.
     02 WS-PR-GRADE      PIC 99.
     02 WS-PR-AGE        PIC 999.
     02 WS-PR-GENDER     PIC X.
     02 WS-PR-REFNO      PIC 9999.
     02 WS-PR-ADDR       PIC X(30).
```

```
      02  WS-PR-EMPDATE.
          03  WS-PR-YY      PIC 99.
          03  WS-PR-MM      PIC 99.
          03  WS-PR-DD    PIC 99.
      02  WS-PR-PAY       PIC 9(6)V99.
      02  WS-PR-BONUS       PIC 9(6)V99.
      02  WS-PR-CAR       PIC X(20).


  01   WS-CV-RECORD.
      02  WS-PR-NAME      PIC X(20).
      02  WS-PR-EMPNO       PIC X(8).
      02  WS-PR-EMPTYPE   PIC X.
      02  WS-PR-GRADE       PIC 99.
      02  WS-PR-AGE       PIC 999.
      02  WS-PR-GENDER    PIC X.
      02  WS-PR-REFNO       PIC 9999.
      02  WS-PR-ADDR      PIC X(30).
      02  WS-CV-EMPDATE.
          03  WS-CV-CC    PIC 99.
          03  WS-PR-YY    PIC 99.
          03  WS-PR-MM    PIC 99.
          03  WS-PR-DD    PIC 99.
      02  WS-PR-PAY       PIC 9(6)V99.
      02  WS-PR-BONUS       PIC 9(6)V99.
      02  WS-PR-CAR       PIC X(20).


  01   WS-TODAY.
      02  WS-TODAY-YY       PIC 99.
      02  WS-TODAY-MM       PIC 99.
      02  WS-TODAY-DD       PIC 99.
  01   WS-I-FRONT        PIC 99 VALUE 88.
  01   WS-I-HORIZON      PIC 9999.
  01   WS-I-END-FILE     PIC X VALUE "N".
  01   WS-I-PR-STATUS    PIC XX.

 PROCEDURE DIVISION.
 A-MAIN-LINE SECTION.
 A-000-MAIN.
     PERFORM AA-INITIALISE.
     READ I-PAYROLL-MASTER AT END
     MOVE "Y" TO WS-I-END-FILE.
     PERFORM AB-PROCESS UNTIL WS-I-END-FILE = "Y".
     PERFORM AC-TERMINATE.

 A-999-EXIT.
     STOP RUN.
```

```
AA-INITIALISE SECTION.
AA-000-OPEN.
    OPEN INPUT I-PAYROLL-MASTER.
    IF WS-I-PR-STATUS NOT EQUAL ZERO THEN
        DISPLAY "Error " WS-I-PR-STATUS
            " opening employee master file."
        GO TO A-999-EXIT
    END-IF.
AA-999-EXIT.
    EXIT.


AB-PROCESS SECTION.
AB-000-MOVE-DATA.
    MOVE I-PR-RECORD TO WS-PR-RECORD.
    MOVE ZEROS TO WS-PR-REFNO OF WS-PR-RECORD.
    MOVE CORRESPONDING WS-PR-RECORD TO WS-CV-RECORD.
    MOVE CORRESPONDING WS-PR-EMPDATE TO WS-CV-EMPDATE.


AB-010-CONVERT-DATA.
    ACCEPT WS-TODAY FROM DATE.
    DISPLAY WS-TODAY.
    ADD WS-I-FRONT TO WS-TODAY-YY GIVING WS-I-HORIZON.
    IF WS-I-HORIZON > 100
        SUBTRACT 100 FROM WS-I-HORIZON.
    IF WS-PR-YY OF WS-PR-RECORD > WS-I-HORIZON
        MOVE 19 TO WS-CV-CC
    ELSE
        MOVE 20 TO WS-CV-CC
    END-IF.


AB-020-DISPLAY-CONVERTED.
    DISPLAY WS-CV-RECORD.


AB-030-READ-DATA.
    READ I-PAYROLL-MASTER AT END
        MOVE "Y" TO WS-I-END-FILE.


AB-999-EXIT.
    EXIT.


AC-TERMINATE SECTION.
AC-000-CLOSE.
    CLOSE I-PAYROLL-MASTER.


AC-999-EXIT.
    EXIT.
```

Here, only one file – `SEQPMAST.DAT` – is defined. The program reads it record by record and interprets the date that each record holds. The contents of `SEQPMAST.DAT` on input are:

```
Conor Sexton        1234    C10029M    Rathfarnham, Dublin,
Ireland. 9511090100000000000000Bubble Car       Mike Cash
2345       S25039M       Jordan Hill, Oxford, UK.
8712120500000000500000Ferrari Testarossa Rebecca Hammersley
5643       S10023F       Summertown, Oxford, UK.
9601010250000000250000E-type Jag       Neil Fawcet
0089       S29045M       Blenheim, Oxford, UK.
8504010900000001000000Mercedes S600
```

The dates are clearly in the 6-digit, pre-Y2K, format. In the program, the lines:

```
01  WS-I-FRONT      PIC 99 VALUE 88.
01  WS-I-HORIZON  PIC 9999.
```

define the range of the sliding window as being 88 years from the year in the current system date and 12 years before that year. In fact, 88 is a somewhat unlikely number to select as the forward displacement; 40 or 50 would be more common. However, a displacement of 88, for illustrative purposes, suits the dates stored in `SEQPMAST.DAT`. If the current year is 1998 (98), the 'horizon' of the sliding window range is calculated to be 86 (98 + 88 – 100). If the year read from the file (say 95) is greater than that horizon, it is prefixed with '19' (1995); otherwise (say 85), it is prefixed with '20' (2085). The critical code in the program is this:

```
AB-010-CONVERT-DATA.
    ACCEPT WS-TODAY FROM DATE.
    DISPLAY WS-TODAY.
    ADD WS-I-FRONT TO WS-TODAY-YY GIVING WS-I-HORIZON.
    IF WS-I-HORIZON > 100
        SUBTRACT 100 FROM WS-I-HORIZON.
    IF WS-PR-YY OF WS-PR-RECORD > WS-I-HORIZON
        MOVE 19 TO WS-CV-CC
    ELSE
        MOVE 20 TO WS-CV-CC
    END-IF.
```

The current date is accepted from the operating system and is displayed. The horizon is calculated as 86. Dates are interpreted as being in the range 1987 to 2086. Here is the program's output:

```
980823
Conor Sexton        1234    C10029M0000Rathfarnham, Dublin,
Ireland. 19951109010000000000000Bubble Car
980823
Mike Cash           2345    S25039M0000Jordan Hill, Oxford,
UK.      19871212050000000000500000Ferrari Testarossa
980823
Rebecca Hammersley  5643    S10023F0000Summertown, Oxford,
UK.      19960101025000000000250000E-type Jag
980823
Neil Fawcet         0089    S29045M0000Blenheim, Oxford, UK.
20850401090000000001000000Mercedes S600
```

For each record, the current date (980823) is displayed. Within each record, the interpreted dates – 1995, 1987, 1996, 2085 – appear.

The advantages offered by the sliding window technique are:

- Large saving (compared to date-expansion) when processing Class 2 dates

- File formats are unchanged

- Because the horizon moves, the solution is potentially permanent.

Here are some of the drawbacks:

- The technique must be confined to Class 2 dates; any date on file for which the century cannot be inferred must be processed as a Class 1 date using expansion. Care needs to be taken at the inventory and assessment stage of the Y2K project to distinguish between the two types.

- Sorted data, such as that appearing in reports, appears wrongly with, for example, 00 (2000) appearing *before* 87 (1987).

- One 'horizon' must be standardised on to avoid confusion, not just in the organisation that owns the applications to which the sliding window is applied, but also to all third parties with whom data generated by those applications is exchanged.

The advantage conferred by sliding windows – avoiding having to expand dates – is so great that it is widely used despite the drawbacks.

5.4 Fixed windows

Using the alternative windowing form, presented in this section, we set an arbitrary *pivot year*, say 90, representing 1990. Then we simply adopt the convention that all two-digit years greater than or equal to 90 are of the twentieth century – 1994, 1997 and so on – while all those less than 90 are of the 21st century, with the two-digit year being prefixed with '20'. File data, again, is unchanged. Here is the program DATEFWIN.CBL that implements fixed windowing. Because is it similar to DATESWIN.CBL, some of the code at the start is omitted.

```
01   WS-I-PIVOT       PIC 99 VALUE 90.
01   WS-I-END-FILE    PIC X VALUE "N".
01   WS-I-PR-STATUS   PIC XX.

PROCEDURE DIVISION.
A-MAIN-LINE SECTION.
A-000-MAIN.
    PERFORM AA-INITIALISE.
    READ I-PAYROLL-MASTER AT END
        MOVE "Y" TO WS-I-END-FILE.
    PERFORM AB-PROCESS UNTIL WS-I-END-FILE = "Y".
    PERFORM AC-TERMINATE.

A-999-EXIT.
    STOP RUN.

AA-INITIALISE SECTION.
AA-000-OPEN.
    OPEN INPUT I-PAYROLL-MASTER.
    IF WS-I-PR-STATUS NOT EQUAL ZERO THEN
        DISPLAY "Error " WS-I-PR-STATUS
            " opening employee master file."
        GO TO A-999-EXIT
    END-IF.

AA-999-EXIT.
    EXIT.

AB-PROCESS SECTION.
AB-000-MOVE-DATA.
    MOVE I-PR-RECORD TO WS-PR-RECORD.
    MOVE ZEROS TO WS-PR-REFNO OF WS-PR-RECORD.
```

```
     MOVE CORRESPONDING WS-PR-RECORD TO WS-CV-RECORD.
     MOVE CORRESPONDING WS-PR-EMPDATE TO WS-CV-EMPDATE.
     IF WS-PR-YY OF WS-PR-RECORD < WS-I-PIVOT
         MOVE 20 TO WS-CV-CC
     ELSE
         MOVE 19 TO WS-CV-CC
     END-IF.

AB-010-DISPLAY-CONVERTED.
     DISPLAY WS-CV-RECORD.

AB-020-READ-DATA.
     READ I-PAYROLL-MASTER AT END
         MOVE "Y" TO WS-I-END-FILE.

AB-999-EXIT.
     EXIT.

AC-TERMINATE SECTION.
AC-000-CLOSE.
     CLOSE I-PAYROLL-MASTER.

AC-999-EXIT.
     EXIT.
```

Here, we define a 'pivot' data item called WS-I-PIVOT and initialise it with the value 90. This is the critical processing:

```
AB-000-MOVE-DATA.
     MOVE I-PR-RECORD TO WS-PR-RECORD.
     MOVE ZEROS TO WS-PR-REFNO OF WS-PR-RECORD.
     MOVE CORRESPONDING WS-PR-RECORD TO WS-CV-RECORD.
     MOVE CORRESPONDING WS-PR-EMPDATE TO WS-CV-EMPDATE.
     IF WS-PR-YY OF WS-PR-RECORD < WS-I-PIVOT
         MOVE 20 TO WS-CV-CC
     ELSE
         MOVE 19 TO WS-CV-CC
     END-IF.
```

The subordinate data items of the input holding area, WS-PR-RECORD are moved to the subordinate data items of WS-CV-RECORD that have the same name. If a name does not match, the contents of the data item are not moved. If the input year is less than the pivot, it is treated as being of the 21st century, otherwise of the 20th century.

The displayed output (again, there is no output file) is this:

```
Conor Sexton         1234    C10029M0000Rathfarnham, Dublin,
Ireland. 199511090100000000000000Bubble Car
Mike Cash            2345    S25039M0000Jordan Hill, Oxford,
UK.        208712120500000000500000Ferrari Testarossa
Rebecca Hammersley  5643     S10023F0000Summertown, Oxford,
UK.        199601010250000000250000E-type Jag
Neil Fawcet          0089    S29045M0000Blenheim, Oxford, UK.
208504010900000001000000Mercedes S600
```

With the pivot of 90, the 1985 and 1987 employment dates of Messrs. Fawcetand Cash have been converted (in memory only, not on file) to the 21st century, while the others remain in the 20th century.

Fixed date windowing, as compared with the sliding window technique shown in the last section, has the disadvantage that the year-range does not move. Eventually, the limit will be reached, with consequences similar to those of the Year 2000 problem today. On the other hand, it has the advantage that, as each year passes, and the system date is incremented, a year's files at the start of the range are not effectively lost. With sliding windows, if the start of the range is 1987 and files are written with two-digit, 87, dates, then next year those dates will be interpreted as 2087. Otherwise, fixed windows shares all the same advantages and disadvantages as sliding windows.

5.5 Date compression

The two-digit year part of a pre-Y2K date can be used to store an encoded form of the year allowing a date range that extends beyond 2000. This encoding is the basis of the techniques presented in this section and in the next.

With date compression, a number system other than decimal is adopted so that the two year digits can store a greater range of years than 00 to 99. Many schemes are possible, but the one most commonly used is to represent the date in hexadecimal (base 16).

This allows a 256-year range to be stored, with the 256 years being calculated forward from a base year, usually chosen as 1900. The actual final year in this scheme is 2155.

Date compression, like windowing, has the advantage over date expansion that no change need be made to file formats. In addition, the century-year combination can be explicitly represented in two digits. This provides a means of *handling Class 1 dates without file expansion*; the compression scheme can also be used for Class 2 dates. Here is a version of the payroll program, DATEHEX.CBL, which implements the date compression technique.

```
*******************************************************************
*                                                                 *
*                     DATEHEX.CBL                                 *
*                                                                 *
*   This program reads the payroll master file and filters date   *
*   information using a compresses (hexadecimal) year value.      *
*   File organization is sequential.                             *
*                                                                 *
*******************************************************************
 IDENTIFICATION DIVISION.
 PROGRAM-ID. DATEHEX.

 ENVIRONMENT DIVISION.

 INPUT-OUTPUT SECTION.
 FILE-CONTROL.
     SELECT OPTIONAL I-PAYROLL-MASTER
     ASSIGN TO "SEQPMAST.DAT"
     ORGANIZATION IS SEQUENTIAL
     ACCESS MODE IS SEQUENTIAL
     FILE STATUS IS WS-I-PR-STATUS.

 DATA DIVISION.
 FILE SECTION.
 FD  I-PAYROLL-MASTER
     BLOCK CONTAINS 20 RECORDS
     LABEL RECORDS ARE STANDARD
     RECORD CONTAINS 111 CHARACTERS.
 01  I-PR-RECORD.
     02 FILLER          PIC X(111).
```

```
WORKING-STORAGE SECTION.
01   WS-PR-RECORD.
     02 WS-PR-NAME              PIC X(20).
     02 WS-PR-EMPNO             PIC X(8).
     02 WS-PR-EMPTYPE           PIC X.
     02 WS-PR-GRADE             PIC 99.
     02 WS-PR-AGE               PIC 999.
     02 WS-PR-GENDER            PIC X.
     02 WS-PR-REFNO             PIC 9999.
     02 WS-PR-ADDR              PIC X(30).
     02 WS-PR-EMPDATE.
        03 WS-PR-YY             PIC XX.
        03 WS-PR-YY-DIGIT REDEFINES WS-PR-YY.
           04 WS-PR-YY-L  PIC X.
           04 WS-PR-YY-R  PIC X.
        03 WS-PR-MM             PIC 99.
        03 WS-PR-DD             PIC 99.
     02 WS-PR-PAY               PIC 9(6)V99.
     02 WS-PR-BONUS             PIC 9(6)V99.
     02 WS-PR-CAR               PIC X(20).

01   WS-CV-RECORD.
     02 WS-PR-NAME              PIC X(20).
     02 WS-PR-EMPNO             PIC X(8).
     02 WS-PR-EMPTYPE           PIC X.
     02 WS-PR-GRADE             PIC 99.
     02 WS-PR-AGE               PIC 999.
     02 WS-PR-GENDER            PIC X.
     02 WS-PR-REFNO             PIC 9999.
     02 WS-PR-ADDR              PIC X(30).
     02 WS-CV-EMPDATE.
        03 WS-CV-YY             PIC 9999.
        03 WS-PR-MM             PIC 99.
        03 WS-PR-DD             PIC 99.
     02 WS-PR-PAY               PIC 9(6)V99.
     02 WS-PR-BONUS             PIC 9(6)V99.
     02 WS-PR-CAR               PIC X(20).

01   WS-I-BASE-YEAR            PIC 9999 VALUE 1900.
01   WS-I-END-FILE            PIC X VALUE "N".
01   WS-I-PR-STATUS           PIC XX.

PROCEDURE DIVISION.
A-MAIN-LINE SECTION.
A-000-MAIN.
     PERFORM AA-INITIALISE.
     READ I-PAYROLL-MASTER AT END
         MOVE "Y" TO WS-I-END-FILE.
```

```
     PERFORM AB-PROCESS UNTIL WS-I-END-FILE = "Y".
     PERFORM AC-TERMINATE.

A-999-EXIT.
     STOP RUN.

AA-INITIALISE SECTION.
AA-000-OPEN.
     OPEN INPUT I-PAYROLL-MASTER.
     IF WS-I-PR-STATUS NOT EQUAL ZERO THEN
         DISPLAY "Error " WS-I-PR-STATUS
             " opening employee master file."
         GO TO A-999-EXIT
     END-IF.

AA-999-EXIT.
     EXIT.

AB-PROCESS SECTION.
AB-000-MOVE-DATA.
     MOVE I-PR-RECORD TO WS-PR-RECORD.
     MOVE ZEROS TO WS-PR-REFNO OF WS-PR-RECORD.
     MOVE CORRESPONDING WS-PR-RECORD TO WS-CV-RECORD.
     MOVE CORRESPONDING WS-PR-EMPDATE TO WS-CV-EMPDATE.
     MOVE WS-I-BASE-YEAR TO WS-CV-YY.
     PERFORM ABA-CONVERT-DATE.

AB-010-DISPLAY-CONVERTED.
     DISPLAY WS-CV-RECORD.

AB-020-READ-DATA.
     READ I-PAYROLL-MASTER AT END
         MOVE "Y" TO WS-I-END-FILE.

AB-999-EXIT.
     EXIT.

ABA-CONVERT-DATE SECTION.
ABA-000-CONVERT-DIGIT-LEFT.
     EVALUATE WS-PR-YY-L
         WHEN '1' ADD 16 TO WS-CV-YY
         WHEN '2' ADD 32 TO WS-CV-YY
         WHEN '3' ADD 48 TO WS-CV-YY
         WHEN '4' ADD 64 TO WS-CV-YY
         WHEN '5' ADD 80 TO WS-CV-YY
         WHEN '6' ADD 96 TO WS-CV-YY
         WHEN '7' ADD 112 TO WS-CV-YY
         WHEN '8' ADD 128 TO WS-CV-YY
         WHEN '9' ADD 144 TO WS-CV-YY
```

```
              WHEN 'A' ADD 160 TO WS-CV-YY
              WHEN 'B' ADD 176 TO WS-CV-YY
              WHEN 'C' ADD 192 TO WS-CV-YY
              WHEN 'D' ADD 208 TO WS-CV-YY
              WHEN 'E' ADD 224 TO WS-CV-YY
              WHEN 'F' ADD 240 TO WS-CV-YY
          END-EVALUATE.

    ABA-010-CONVERT-DIGIT-RIGHT.
          EVALUATE WS-PR-YY-R
              WHEN '1' ADD 1 TO WS-CV-YY
              WHEN '2' ADD 2 TO WS-CV-YY
              WHEN '3' ADD 3 TO WS-CV-YY
              WHEN '4' ADD 4 TO WS-CV-YY
              WHEN '5' ADD 5 TO WS-CV-YY
              WHEN '6' ADD 6 TO WS-CV-YY
              WHEN '7' ADD 7 TO WS-CV-YY
              WHEN '8' ADD 8 TO WS-CV-YY
              WHEN '9' ADD 9 TO WS-CV-YY
              WHEN 'A' ADD 10 TO WS-CV-YY
              WHEN 'B' ADD 11 TO WS-CV-YY
              WHEN 'C' ADD 12 TO WS-CV-YY
              WHEN 'D' ADD 13 TO WS-CV-YY
              WHEN 'E' ADD 14 TO WS-CV-YY
              WHEN 'F' ADD 15 TO WS-CV-YY
          END-EVALUATE.

    ABA-999-EXIT.
          EXIT.

    AC-TERMINATE SECTION.
    AC-000-CLOSE.
          CLOSE I-PAYROLL-MASTER.

    AC-999-EXIT.
          EXIT.
```

As with the windowing techniques, compression does not produce an output file; it merely interprets the date in code. That date is represented as two hexadecimal digits where, for example, hexadecimal 21 is decimal 33, hexadecimal 4A is decimal 74 and hexadecimal FE is decimal 254. A major part of DATEHEX.CBL is COBOL code for converting hexadecimal year representations read from file to their decimal equivalent for use while the program is in execution.

The base year is set in this data definition:

```
01  WS-I-BASE-YEAR      PIC 9999 VALUE 1900.
```

The critical piece of code is this:

```
AB-000-MOVE-DATA.
    MOVE I-PR-RECORD TO WS-PR-RECORD.
    MOVE ZEROS TO WS-PR-REFNO OF WS-PR-RECORD.
    MOVE CORRESPONDING WS-PR-RECORD TO WS-CV-RECORD.
    MOVE CORRESPONDING WS-PR-EMPDATE TO WS-CV-EMPDATE.
    MOVE WS-I-BASE-YEAR TO WS-CV-YY.
PERFORM ABA-CONVERT-DATE.
```

As usual, the input record is moved to its holding area in memory. Each item from that area is moved to the item in the converted ('CV') area that has the same name. 1900 is assigned as a base year. This followed by the conversion from hexadecimal to decimal, which is done separately on the left and right characters of the input YY hexadecimal representation.

The state of the input file SEQPMAST.DAT when DATEHEX.CBL starts execution is this:

```
Conor Sexton         1234    C10029M    Rathfarnham, Dublin,
Ireland. FE110901000000000000000Bubble Car        Mike Cash
2345        S25039M        Jordan  Hill,  Oxford,  UK.
8712120500000000500000Ferrari Testarossa Rebecca Hammersley
5643        S10023F        Summertown,  Oxford,  UK.
9601010250000000250000E-type  Jag              Neil Fawcet
0089        S29045M         Blenheim,  Oxford,  UK.
8504010900000000100000Mercedes  S600
```

My record holds the date FE1109; the year obviously needs conversion to decimal. This is the displayed output of DATEHEX.CBL when it runs:

```
Conor Sexton         1234    C10029M0000Rathfarnham, Dublin,
Ireland. 2154110901000000000000000Bubble  Car
Mike Cash            2345    S25039M0000Jordan Hill, Oxford,
UK.      2035121205000000000500000Ferrari  Testarossa
Rebecca Hammersley  5643    S10023F0000Summertown, Oxford,
UK.      2050010102500000000250000E-type  Jag
Neil Fawcet          0089    S29045M0000Blenheim, Oxford, UK.
2033040109000000001000000Mercedes  S600
```

Here, my record has been interpreted as holding the (decimal) year 2154. Note that the other years have been converted also. For example, Mr. Cash's year, input as 87, has been interpreted as 1900 + (8 × 16) + 7 = 2035.

The advantages offered by the date compression technique are:

- It can handle Class 1 dates without date expansion.

- It handles Class 2 dates also.

- File record size is unchanged.

- Date comparisons can be done directly, if all dates have been compressed.

The disadvantages of date compression are these:

- The values used to represent dates are counter-intuitive: most people do not see the year 2154 in 'FE'.

- Existing data must be converted.

- All parties sharing affected applications and data files must agree on the compression format.

- Existing date-validation code is badly affected by date compression. Given the enormous amount of such code in existence, this is a real problem.

At first sight, compression gives the important benefit that file-expansion can be avoided altogether, even for Class 1 dates. However, all the dates in all files would have to be converted before being used. The main reason why this is a minority technique is the aspect of obscurity and of having to explain and agree the format with many other parties.

5.6 Date encoding

Date encoding involves assignment of a special meaning to date data stored on file such that one form will be interpreted as the 20th century and the other form as the 21st. The technique shown here allows 6-digit, pre-Y2K, dates to cover the whole of the 20th and 21st centuries. As with compression, the century information is explicitly stored without the need for date expansion. As with compression also, the gain is offset somewhat by a relative lack of clarity of the technique in operation.

In a six-digit date, the month field is restricted to a value between 1 and 12, inclusive of both. We can encode the month field such that dates stored with months in the range 1-12 are interpreted as being 20th century dates, while those with a fixed added factor, say 50, are regarded as being of the 21st century. For example, month 11 is November. By adding 50, a 21st century November would be stored as 61 and interpreted accordingly.

The program that implements this conversion is very much the same as earlier versions of the payroll application. Only the important latter part of DATECODE.CBL follows:

```
01   WS-I-SHIFT        PIC 99 VALUE 50.
01   WS-I-END-FILE     PIC X VALUE "N".
01   WS-I-PR-STATUS    PIC XX.

PROCEDURE DIVISION.
A-MAIN-LINE SECTION.
A-000-MAIN.
    PERFORM AA-INITIALISE.
    READ I-PAYROLL-MASTER AT END
        MOVE "Y" TO WS-I-END-FILE.
    PERFORM AB-PROCESS UNTIL WS-I-END-FILE = "Y".
    PERFORM AC-TERMINATE.

A-999-EXIT.
    STOP RUN.

AA-INITIALISE SECTION.
AA-000-OPEN.
    OPEN INPUT I-PAYROLL-MASTER.
    IF WS-I-PR-STATUS NOT EQUAL ZERO THEN
        DISPLAY "Error " WS-I-PR-STATUS
            " opening employee master file."
        GO TO A-999-EXIT
    END-IF.
```

5.6 Date encoding

```
AA-999-EXIT.
    EXIT.

AB-PROCESS SECTION.
AB-000-MOVE-DATA.
    MOVE I-PR-RECORD TO WS-PR-RECORD.
    MOVE ZEROS TO WS-PR-REFNO OF WS-PR-RECORD.
    MOVE CORRESPONDING WS-PR-RECORD TO WS-CV-RECORD.
    MOVE CORRESPONDING WS-PR-EMPDATE TO WS-CV-EMPDATE.
    IF WS-PR-MM OF WS-CV-RECORD > 12
        MOVE 20 TO WS-CV-CC
        SUBTRACT WS-I-SHIFT FROM WS-PR-MM OF WS-CV-RECORD
    ELSE
        MOVE 19 TO WS-CV-CC
    END-IF.

AB-010-DISPLAY-CONVERTED.
    DISPLAY WS-CV-RECORD.

AB-020-READ-DATA.
    READ I-PAYROLL-MASTER AT END
        MOVE "Y" TO WS-I-END-FILE.

AB-999-EXIT.
    EXIT.

AC-TERMINATE SECTION.
AC-000-CLOSE.
    CLOSE I-PAYROLL-MASTER.

AC-999-EXIT.
    EXIT.
```

Again, there is no output to file: the date-conversion process is 'on the fly' and done only in the system's memory. If the input year is in the upper range (51-62) - generated by adding WS-I-SHIFT - the whole date is treated as a 21st century one.

Assuming that the input file, SEQPMAST.DAT, contains a month-encoded date, 956109, in its first record, the displayed output from this program appears as follows:

```
Conor Sexton       1234    C10029M0000Rathfarnham, Dublin,
Ireland. 2095110901000000000000000Bubble Car
Mike Cash          2345    S25039M0000Jordan Hill, Oxford,
UK.      1987121205000000000500000Ferrari Testarossa
```

```
Rebecca Hammersley  5643    S10023F0000Summertown, Oxford,
UK.        19960101025000000250000E-type Jag
Neil Fawcet        0089    S29045M0000Blenheim, Oxford, UK.
198504010900000001000000Mercedes S600
```

My record from the file has been changed in memory to contain the year 2095 in its date.

The advantages and disadvantages of date encoding are much the same as those that apply to compression, the major objections being counter-intuitiveness and the effect on date-validation code.

5.7 Bridges

Bridges are filter programs, and are crucial tools in maintaining compatibility between date-expanded, Y2K-converted files and applications that have not yet been Y2K-repaired. A filter program in general converts one data format to another; in the case of Y2K, the requirement is for conversion between 6-digit and 8-digit date formats. Filters can be bidirectional, but I strongly recommend that any bridges your organisation might write as part of its Y2K project should convert in one direction only: from expanded 8-digit dates back to 6-digit pre-Y2K dates. Doing this makes your newly date-expanded files in effect read-only as far as the bridge program is concerned. By keeping the conversion one-way, you sharply reduce the scope for error and for corruption of the expanded files.

The purpose of one-directional Y2K bridges is to allow applications that have not been Y2K-repaired to use the same file data – other than the expanded dates. Something of a myth prevails that bridges should be of limited life-span: that eventually all applications will be converted and the bridges will become obsolete and be discarded. This kind of thinking – with 'temporary' code written in the 1960s – led to the Y2K problem in the first place. If a bridge is in place, allowing a non-Y2K-clean application to run, this may become the status quo. Once a bridge comes into existence in your organisation, do not assume that it will easily go away.

The program BRIDGE.CBL takes as input the file SEQPEXP.DAT – with the dates expanded – and 'strips it down' to its original 6-digit-year format. It produces as output the file SEQPFILT.DAT, the contents of which are the same as the original payroll input file SEQPMAST.DAT. Here is the program:

```
*********************************************************************
*                                                                   *
*                         BRIDGE.CBL                                 *
*                                                                   *
*  This program reads the date-expanded payroll master file and     *
*  filters its contents to produce the equivalent pre-Y2K file       *
*  with two-digit years in date fields.                             *
*                                                                   *
*********************************************************************
 IDENTIFICATION DIVISION.
 PROGRAM-ID. BRIDGE.

 ENVIRONMENT DIVISION.

 INPUT-OUTPUT SECTION.
 FILE-CONTROL.
     SELECT OPTIONAL I-PAYROLL-EXPAND
     ASSIGN TO "SEQPEXP.DAT"
     ORGANIZATION IS SEQUENTIAL
     ACCESS MODE IS SEQUENTIAL
     FILE STATUS IS WS-I-PR-STATUS.

     SELECT OPTIONAL O-PAYROLL-FILTER
     ASSIGN TO "SEQPFILT.DAT"
     ORGANIZATION IS SEQUENTIAL
     ACCESS MODE IS SEQUENTIAL
     FILE STATUS IS WS-O-PR-STATUS.

 DATA DIVISION.
 FILE SECTION.
 FD  I-PAYROLL-EXPAND
     BLOCK CONTAINS 20 RECORDS
     LABEL RECORDS ARE STANDARD
     RECORD CONTAINS 119 CHARACTERS.
 01  I-PR-RECORD.
     02 FILLER           PIC X(119).

 FD  O-PAYROLL-FILTER
     BLOCK CONTAINS 20 RECORDS
     LABEL RECORDS ARE STANDARD
```

```
          RECORD CONTAINS 111 CHARACTERS.
01   O-PR-RECORD.
     02 FILLER              PIC X(111).

WORKING-STORAGE SECTION.
01   WS-I-END-FILE      PIC X VALUE "N".
01   WS-I-PR-STATUS     PIC XX.
01   WS-O-PR-STATUS     PIC XX.

PROCEDURE DIVISION.
A-MAIN-LINE SECTION.
A-000-MAIN.
     PERFORM AA-INITIALISE.
     READ I-PAYROLL-EXPAND AT END
         MOVE "Y" TO WS-I-END-FILE.
     PERFORM AB-PROCESS UNTIL WS-I-END-FILE = "Y".
     PERFORM AC-TERMINATE.

A-999-EXIT.
     STOP RUN.

AA-INITIALISE SECTION.
AA-000-OPEN.
     OPEN INPUT I-PAYROLL-EXPAND.
     IF WS-I-PR-STATUS NOT EQUAL ZERO THEN
         DISPLAY "Error " WS-I-PR-STATUS
             " opening expanded-date file."
         GO TO A-999-EXIT
     END-IF.

     OPEN OUTPUT O-PAYROLL-FILTER.
     IF WS-O-PR-STATUS NOT EQUAL ZERO THEN
         DISPLAY "Error " WS-O-PR-STATUS
             " opening output-filter file."
         GO TO A-999-EXIT
     END-IF.
AA-999-EXIT.
     EXIT.

AB-PROCESS SECTION.
AB-000-FILTER-DATA.
     WRITE O-PR-RECORD FROM I-PR-RECORD.
     IF WS-O-PR-STATUS NOT EQUAL ZERO THEN
         DISPLAY "Error " WS-O-PR-STATUS
             " writing filtered-date file."
         GO TO A-999-EXIT
     END-IF.
```

```
AB-010-READ-DATA.
    READ I-PAYROLL-EXPAND AT END
        MOVE "Y" TO WS-I-END-FILE.

AB-999-EXIT.
    EXIT.


AC-TERMINATE SECTION.
AC-000-CLOSE.
    CLOSE I-PAYROLL-EXPAND.
    CLOSE O-PAYROLL-FILTER.

AC-999-EXIT.
    EXIT.
```

BRIDGE.CBL reads the date-expanded file SEQPEXP.DAT and converts it 'back' to SEQPFILT.DAT. The input file has these contents:

```
Conor Sexton        1234    C10029M0000Rathfarnham, Dublin,
Ireland. 95110901000000000000000Bubble Car        19951109Mike
Cash        2345    S25039M0000Jordan Hill, Oxford, UK.
87121205000000000500000Ferrari Testarossa  19871212Rebecca
Hammersley  5643    S10023F0000Summertown, Oxford, UK.
96010102500000000250000E-type Jag        19960101Neil
Fawcet      0089    S29045M0000Blenheim, Oxford, UK.
85040109000000001000000Mercedes S600        19850401
```

As with the original date-expanded file SEQPCONV.DAT produced by the program DATECONV.CBL, expanded dates are appended to the end of each file record. The contents of the file, SEQPFILT.DAT, output by BRIDGE.CBL, are these:

```
Conor Sexton        1234    C10029M0000Rathfarnham, Dublin,
Ireland. 95110901000000000000000Bubble Car        Mike Cash
2345        S25039M0000Jordan  Hill,  Oxford,  UK.
87121205000000000500000Ferrari Testarossa Rebecca Hammersley
5643        S10023F0000Summertown,  Oxford,  UK.
96010102500000000250000E-type Jag        Neil Fawcet
0089        S29045M0000Blenheim,  Oxford,  UK.
85040109000000001000000Mercedes S600
```

The expanded dates have disappeared and the file is back to the original pre-Y2K format. The bridge program is unremarkable but it has one crucial feature that could go by unnoticed: it takes advantage of the fact that the expanded date was appended to the end of each record in the expanded file. Up to that date field, the format of all the records in the expanded file is identical to the record format in the original file. This means that, instead of having to 'pick around' in the individual record data items, BRIDGE.CBL can do a very simple copy:

```
 AB-000-FILTER-DATA.
WRITE O-PR-RECORD FROM I-PR-RECORD.
IF WS-O-PR-STATUS NOT EQUAL ZERO THEN
    DISPLAY "Error " WS-O-PR-STATUS
        " writing filtered-date file."
    GO TO A-999-EXIT
END-IF.
```

This writes to the 'stripped down', pre-Y2K-format, record from an expanded record. Because of where the expanded date field is, the expanded date 'falls off the end' automatically and is not included in the output record. An additional benefit of the simple copy is that the temporary record holding areas in the WORKING-STORAGE section are not needed and are omitted.

The moral of the tale here is that a 6-digit date field in a file record should never be replaced in the record definition by an expanded date field. Appending the expanded dates, as shown, greatly simplifies bridge programs that must process them.

5.8 Code search considerations

Regardless of the kind of application your organisation is dealing with, the specific date operations that you will need to be aware of include these:

- Calculations and sorting based on dates retrieved from databases and files.

- Generation of the system date – for example, the COBOL-85 (the most common COBOL standard, to which many applications adhere) DATE call is not Y2K-clean.

- Date conversions: code that changes dates from the North American MM/DD/ (CC) YY to the European DD/MM/ (CC) YY and back; conversion between Gregorian and Julian dates; change from DD/MM/ (CC) YY to (CC) YY/MM/DD for sorting purposes.

- Dates to be sorted: year 2000 represented as 00 will precede all other years.

- Date validation.

- Julian – YYDDD format – dates (see Chapter 1).

- Dates to be subtracted for date-ageing: a pensioner born in 1904 could in 2000 receive a notice to start kindergarten!

Most Y2K projects have settled on a combination of date expansion (for Class 1 dates) and sliding windows (for Class 2 dates) as the strategy that best satisfies these requirements. Expansion is expensive, but sorting, arithmetic and validation will work with the resulting dates. For all their clever attractiveness in potentially avoiding date expansion, the compression and encoding schemes cause a real difficulty here. If compression is excluded from consideration, then some dates will have to be expanded. However, the proportion of dates in typical files that actually *must* be expanded is small: estimates vary around 10%.

The crucial tactics that I have pointed out, which will save much unnecessary effort if applied, are these:

- After identifying them, ignore Class 3 dates.

- Do date expansion for Class 1 dates *only*.

- Use windowing for all other (Class 2) dates.

- Never replace a 6-digit date field with an expanded equivalent; put the new definition at the end of the existing record.

The key to executing these recommendations is being able to identify dates and date operations in the first place. For this, your organisation will need a good search tool, of which many are available, for COBOL and other languages. Most give in the region of a 90–95% success rate in their search and will optionally fix the code as well. Claims of enabling one programmer to Y2K-repair 100,000 lines of code a week seem excessive, but the jump-start provided by the tools makes them indispensable. Refer to your organisation's supplier, or to the Web sites I mention in this chapter and in Chapter 7, for details on specific products.

Finally, remember that no matter how good your chosen search-and-fix tool, it will not catch all date-dependencies in your code. The Y2K work plan must therefore build in enough time for all code to be manually checked and changed.

6 | Test and migration

6.1 Testing client workstations

As I have by now repeatedly noted, the hard part of Y2K is not repairing and testing application software on mainframe or server systems; it is getting (usually PC) client workstations to a consistent Y2K-clean state with hardware, operating system, communications and application software tested, and accepted by the end-user. The organisation must (as part of the Inventory phase) identify the distinct PC configurations it supports. The components that make the distinction are usually the PC's network card and sometimes the disk drive or video controller. The more standard the organisation's stock of PCs, the easier it is to perform the Y2K upgrade, test and migration. Standardisation of client PCs is so important to maintaining them effectively that many large enterprises today settle on a single PC configuration, which is then periodically upgraded or replaced.

For purposes of testing client PCs for the correctness of the Y2K changes, I will assume that:

- Your organisation – unless it has fewer than 20 or so clients – does not attempt to maintain its PCs purely manually, relying on manual installation of the operating system and network software, followed by ad-hoc loading of applications.

- Your organisation has standardised on one or a very few client PC hardware and software configurations.

- You intend to initialise PCs either using a gold build or over the network using a software deployment utility; the point being that the software environment found on all the organisation's PCs will be consistent.

- Your organisation will have a PC test 'shop', containing representative examples of all real client PC configurations in use. Each of these must be configured with required network software, with connections both to a back-end application server and to network server(s) as is normal for client PCs in the organisation. It is important in this testing context that the application server with which the clients interact is a test system.

If these assumptions are true, then it is possible to carry out the client side of Y2K testing in a limited, off-line and disciplined environment and not – system and network administrators give thanks here – at each of the (200 or 2,000) end-user PC locations. If there is high confidence about the consistency of all the client PCs – they all run either a single gold build, or a very few well-defined ones – Y2K testing can be done on the sample of PCs found in the test 'shop' and its results assumed valid for all the client PCs.

Initialising test PCs

As the first step in testing, a client PC of a configuration standard to the organisation is initialised with operating system, network software and applications, all, we hope, Y2K-clean. The installation is, as explained in Chapter 4, either from a gold build or from deployment over the network. Either way, it is initiated from a boot diskette designed (network cards are particularly in mind here) for that PC configuration. Building PCs in this way can be quite quick: between 15 and 30 minutes is not unusual for a gold build from CD – although this may be slowed if the deployment is over the network.

Date testing the BIOS and operating system

All Y2K testing centres on what happens to the operation of a computer system if the system clock is rolled forward to 2000 or later. It should also continue to function when the clock is rolled back. The tests to be performed on the installed PC are these:

- Verify that the installed gold-build operating system and environment start apparently correctly.

- Perform the BIOS check outlined in Chapter 4. Does the system clock roll over when it is left switched on at midnight, December 31, 1999? If the PC is switched off just before midnight and switched just after, will the new date be January 1, 2000?

- Verify that a file created while the system date is set to 2000 or later has a correct datestamp, and that it is then interpreted properly by the operating system and its utilities.

- Verify that events that should be carried out automatically on the PC – scheduled events such as backups or automated connections with remote systems – work with rolled-forward dates.

- See if any unwanted automated events occur with the date rolled forward and, further, whether or not there is a sudden accumulation of processes that would otherwise be executed at intervals, say monthly, between now and 2000.

- With the date rolled forward, check if any messages appear warning about expired software licences. This may only happen for a licensed application when the attempt is made to start it.

- With the date rolled forward (and assuming a Windows 95/98 or Windows NT/2000 client) verify that you can log out and re-login: that your ID is still recognised and its password has not expired.

- Check that the operating system works with – in terms both of system clock and file datestamps – important boundary dates:

January 1 2000	(the Great Day)
February 29 2000	(valid: 2000 is a leap year)
December 31 2000	(does it roll to January 1, 2001)
February 29 2001	(invalid: not a leap year)
February 29 1900	(invalid: not a leap year)

- Set the date to just before midnight on February 28 2000. Verify that it rolls forward to February 29 2000. Set the time to just before midnight. Check that it rolls forward to March 1 2000.

- Perform the above tests with the PC disconnected from the network. Repeat them with connections to LAN and application servers established. Verify that any timestamp synchronisation being imposed by the servers is done and handled correctly.

- Document any failures that are encountered.

Dates and stand-alone client applications

The above tests are designed to ensure that the PC's CMOS, BIOS and operating system can handle the well-known boundary dates. The same, and some other, tests must be done for both shrink-wrapped and application software that will be part of the standard PC build. Both kinds of application will almost certainly create files or other data containing expanded and windowed dates. Both have, by the time they are installed on one of your organisation's test PCs, been tested stand-alone: in the case of shrink-wrapped programs, by the supplier; home-grown applications by your organisation's software development department.

The job now is to ensure that the applications work in a PC environment representative of the kind found in production. All this must be done repeatedly under a variety of conditions. Here are some suggested tests:

- Ensure that the PC's network connections are down or that the PC is physically disconnected.

- With the PC's system date set to today's (pre-2000) date, verify that all applications start apparently normally. It is not necessary to be conversant with the operation of an application to have a good idea whether or not it has started successfully.

- With the PC's system date rolled forward to January 1, 2000, again try and start the applications.

- Note any messages that appear complaining about expired application licences.

- Where the system date shows as 01/01/00 (January 1, 2000) test that all applications display an unambiguous 4-digit year – either 01/01/1900 or 01/01/2000 – depending on how each application is intended to handle such a date.

- For each application, generate test data, some with dates before 2000, some with dates after. Using the current (pre-2000) system clock, exercise the application with that data.

- For each application, do the same with the system date rolled forward.

- For each application, create test data holding examples of each of the boundary dates specified in the previous list. Also include dates close to the boundary of windows – sliding or fixed – that are used by the applications.

- Run each PC application against each of these dates, verifying that they are correctly processed.

- Document the results of these application tests.

Client/server applications

The set of tests above is designed to verify that, given a functioning PC environment in terms of operating system, network and hardware, applications standard to the organisation will work stand-alone. For some applications, particularly PC front-ends of client/server programs mostly resident on a back-end server or mainframe, stand-alone tests are not very realistic. Usually, the front-end will start, try to establish communications with its server software and, when it fails to do so, halt with a more or less meaningful message.

The focus is now on the client's perspective: to verify that the front-end software runs, and that that software can both access the network and exchange data correctly with its counterpart on the appropriate server. It is difficult to be general about precisely what tests should be carried out on client software without being specific about what it does; a generic example follows.

Let us assume that the software application in question processes transactions in a conventional way, sending New, Delete, and Update transactions to the server for processing and possible return of information. Examples include an on-line payroll or reservations system, and both of these will be writing to and reading from files that store dates in abundance. The following list is a reasonable set of tests that should be applied to the client/server application as a complete entity:

- Ensure that the network connection between the client PC and the application server is established.

- Create test data on both the client and server sides that contains records holding post-1999 dates including the boundary values I have already given.

- Synchronise the clocks of both client and server at today's (pre-2000) date.

- Define a representative set of transactions, to be exchanged in processing with the server.

- By posting the test transactions, verify that the post-1999 dates stored on both the client and server sides are processed correctly.

- Verify that any screen display on the client side, or printed output, appears with correct four-digit years (assuming some dates on file have been expanded) and correctly ordered.

- Document the results of these tests.

- Set the system dates on both the client PC and on the server forward to a post-1999 date and time. Note that, particularly on a large server or mainframe system, changing the date like this is not done lightly. If the server is a test system, any unwanted consequences (for example, scheduled tasks wrongly starting execution) should be recoverable without too much difficulty.

- Having reset both system dates and times, repeat the above tests.

• Reset the client and server system dates and times again, this time making them different: one before and one after the roll-over. Run the transaction tests again.

In the unlikely event of *all* the foregoing tests working without a hitch, the PC is ready for acceptance. Its gold build can now be deployed to all the clients for which it is intended; this is part of the subject of migration, covered later in this chapter.

More commonly, something will fail during all these tests. Assuming the PC system and network software environment is Y2K-clean, the most likely source of trouble with the application software is a failure on the part of the two sides to agree date formats or windowing conventions. There is always the possibility, of course, that some fixes that should have been made to the application code may have been missed. Any such bug means analysing the test results, finding the source of the problem in code, fixing it off-line, compiling, testing the software stand-alone and returning it to the test 'shop'.

6.2 Server test data

We now turn our testing focus to applications resident on the server side of the system. In mainframe environments, this *is* the system. We have seen that, for the client/server application, system testing requires test data and execution concurrently on both the client and server. In a mainframe-centric system, the work is simpler although the volumes of application code and data may be huge.

The input to all application testing is test data. Test data should be designed to exercise and verify the correct operation of the programs that will use it. It should concentrate on exercising and testing those areas of code known to have changed, not all the code. Testing should be precise, targeted and minimised. Given that the test activity often constitutes more than half the overall project effort, the objective of minimising it is an important one, particularly in the context of a project so time-critical as Year 2000.

Test data can be generated in three ways:

- Manually, using an editor or equivalent tool
- With a software utility for generating data. Most of these take as input the definition of a file record and produce instances of the record, populating them with data, including dates spanning Year 2000
- With a program written to do the job.

It is possible to generate very large test data suites with automation provided by the utilities. Most publications, not just those dealing with Y2K, while recognising that exhaustive testing is impossible, recommend generating very large amounts of test data in order to 'fully exercise the code'. This is essentially the blunderbuss approach: fire enough pellets and we'll hit something; we hope everything. It certainly is not analytic.

If as part of the Y2K project, the only software changes made have been changes to code handling dates and to date storage in files, then in principle only that code and data need be tested. An accurate test of the 'issue' at hand ('how does this code behave in finding tomorrow's date where today's is February 28, 2000?') is just as effectively done with a few records of input test data as with a few thousand. Minimal test data should be generated for this and all the other boundary conditions, including test data containing expanded dates.

A problem with very large tests is that they produce very large test results. The clutter can end up obscuring the result you want to see and makes it more rather than less likely that Y2K-related bugs will escape. I have seen this: I know. Based on this rationale, my recommendation is to create a reasonably small test suite, probably using a data generating program developed within your own organisation.

Consider the date classifications I set out in previous chapters: Class 1 requires date expansion and interpretation in code of the century value; Class 2's century value can be derived by context from a two-digit year; and Class 3 dates are harmless. If all the date references in your organisation's applications have been found and classified at the inventory phase, these classifications have clear implications for the amount of testing that must be done on a given application and for the test data that must be generated.

Code that need not be tested

Where a program contains only Class 3 dates, it *need not be modified or tested at all* as part of the Y2K project. This is true where only Y2K date-processing changes are currently being made to applications; if non-Y2K modifications have infiltrated, a program with Class 3 dates only may in fact stop working properly. But, assuming that all changes are purely to dates – field definitions and data and date-processing code – 'Class 3 programs' can be ignored. It is a waste of time to test them or to generate test data for them. Given that these dates are probably in the majority across all applications, this is a very important realisation.

It is sometimes said that COBOL was invented to produce report programs. Not all COBOL report programs, but a very large body of them, *are completely read-only*: they take information in whatever form it appears on file, format it to the desired appearance and print it. It is pointless to apply Y2K fixes to such programs; understanding and identifying this at the inventory and assessment phases will save a great deal of time and money in the execution of your organisation's Y2K project.

Unit test only

Programs that implement only Class 2 or Class 3 dates – that is to say, there is no date expansion – need only be tested stand-alone. Recall from Chapter 5 that all the programs that do one form or another of date windowing, compression or encoding have one identical characteristic: they only ever read date data from file and use program logic to interpret it.

Class 2 dates are never written back to file in their expanded form and they are not used in calculations or sort operations (if they were, they would be Class 1 dates). As such, they only affect the operation of the program to which they belong. Testing can thus be confined to that program. A very high proportion of all dates – 85–90% – are found to be Class 2 and Class 3 dates. Only the balance, therefore, are the genuine, Class 1, expanded dates that can cause so many problems.

Ripple effect

When a date is expanded on file, every entity that subsequently uses it is 'touched' by it. The file formats themselves change as do the screen displays and logic employed by the programs that process the expanded date. The effect of expanded dates obviously does not stop with one program, file or screen. An expanded date may be passed across a sequence of programs. It may be copied to different variables in memory, which may themselves be written to file. In short, every expanded date propagates a 'ripple' effect that must be identified and tracked at the Inventory and Assessment phases.

Good search tools are invaluable in identifying where date expansions are needed and the paths of knock-on effects they initiate. Test data generated for input to programs with Class 1 dates must itself, of course, include expanded dates where necessary. Because expanded dates affect other programs, screens and files in many ways, just to unit test programs containing them is not enough. Such programs must also be integration tested and system tested.

There is one technique that can help reduce testing effort: bridge programs of the type seen in Chapter 5. If we introduce an expanded date into a given program as part of the Y2K project then, in principle, every program that uses a file expanded to contain the date must at least be recompiled and probably changed. Using bridge programs (designed for simplicity with the appended-date technique shown in Chapter 5) allows other programs to work in their original form with the old file format that the bridge effectively converts back to. This also has the effect of making system testing of the changed program simpler and more manageable: a testing situation in which only one program has changed is always better than 'an equation of many variables'.

Test scripts

Finally, in a server environment such as a mainframe or UNIX system, programs are rarely run manually, in sequence, by an operator. Instead, other programs are used to run the applications in the proper sequence automatically and to ensure that the required system resources are available to the programs when they execute. In the mainframe environment, the controlling programs are written in Job Control Language (JCL); the equivalent under UNIX is the 'shell' language. JCL streams (jobstreams) are required on a mainframe to run even the simplest COBOL program, for example. File space must be pre-allocated, files used must be named and printers and other devices allocated to the program. In a client/ server environment with a UNIX system as the back-end, much less effort is needed to schedule the execution of programs. In any case, be it jobstream, shell program or batch file, we must generate 'scripts' to run the testing we require.

6.3 Testing server applications

Preparation

Test preparation consists largely of the activities that are needed to ensure that all the people, equipment, software and other resources that are needed to conduct server application testing are in fact in place. This is not as simple as it seems. Earlier stages in the project – especially test planning – should have identified the applications requiring testing and defined the tests to be executed. Even with test procedure, test data and test scripts available, many other things must happen before testing can begin in earnest.

First, there must be a test system, configured, operational and ready to receive the applications to be tested. It is possible to partition some systems – mainframes in particular – such that a separate 'logical' (not physical) machine for testing resides on the same physical computer as a production system. This will however degrade overall system performance to some degree. In addition, any system programmer or administrator will prefer to keep the test machine physically separate, notwithstanding the supposed security of the partitioning system. Acquisition of a dedicated test server is often a high priority of Y2K projects.

With the test system in place, the next deliverable item is the server applications to be tested. In a client/server environment, delivery of the server software must be co-ordinated with installation of the client components of the application. Any delay in delivery of the application software will impact on the test schedule. Software is always late, it is said, and it is at the interface between the developers and the test team that project schedules often come unstuck.

The application must reach the test team in reasonable condition. It happens surprisingly often that programmers, under pressure to 'integrate' with a version of the application destined for test, will hope for the best and release code that may not even have been successfully compiled. This shows up very quickly when test begins and, causing such a waste of time and effort, is considered one of the worst 'crimes' possible in software development and maintenance.

In addition to test system and application software, the following people and resources must be in place:

- Test staff, with assigned responsibilities

- Test scripts, data and documented 'scenarios'

- Documentation detailing expected test results

- Defined procedures for acceptance or rejection by the test team of the software

- All agreed utilities for generating test data and evaluating test results.

Testing

Testing of server applications (co-operatively with their distributed client components where applicable) is conducted according to the stages outlined in Chapter 3 (section 3.5, Test Plan):

- unit test
- integration test
- system test
- regression test
- acceptance test.

In large installations all testing is executed through these stages; Y2K testing is different in degree in that some steps may deliberately be omitted – recall that programs containing only Class 2 and Class 3 date-dependencies need only be unit tested. Programs affected by files containing expanded dates, on the other hand, must be regression tested to ensure they remain operational after integration of a program that writes to such files. For a client/server application, most testing will be conducted from the client side as outlined at the start of this chapter.

Applications are said to be 'promoted' from unit test through acceptance test. During this process, many other kinds of tests are implicitly or explicitly done of the software and its operation:

- Operations testing: determines whether or not the software is ready for normal production operations, or is so unstable that its place is in the development laboratory.

- Error-condition testing: checks the robustness of the software when it encounters an error condition.

- Usability testing: checks whether or not the human interface – data entry screens, reports and so on – is easy and intuitive to grasp.

- Stress testing: verifies that the software can process realistic loads found in the production environment.

- Requirements testing: checks that the software performs its function correctly over an extended period.

These aspects are verified as part of Y2K testing but, if no new functionality is introduced other than expanded dates and date-handling code, most of the testing effort lies in unit testing and regression testing. In a real test environment, distinction is often not made between the formally-defined phases. For example, testing the interaction of client and server software is by definition not unit testing, but integration and system testing combined.

Y2K testing for applications on a server is the same in principle as that already explained for clients. By varying the system date and populating files used by the applications with newly expanded dates, we verify that the applications function correctly, producing expected, pre-defined results. All the same boundary dates should be used to both to populate the files and in setting the system date. An addition that may be of interest is to check how the applications handle September 9, 1999, the 'all-nines' day.

Each test operative must have an exclusive area (catalog or directory) on the test system, containing the application being tested, libraries and data files. This area is locked to everyone but that tester, and especially to development. When the tester releases the program from test, it is promoted to directories corresponding to integration test, system test and regression test, until finally the application as a whole is released for integration into the production system.

The job of the tester in unit test is to load the test data files and run the planned tests by executing the pre-prepared test script. Then, the tester compares the test outcome – file data, displays, printed output – with the documentation containing the expected results. Where there is a difference constituting a code error, the tester returns the module to development with a description of the symptoms. If the test is error-free, it is promoted to integration test.

After unit test, a program containing only Class 2 and Class 3 dates can be promoted for integration into the production system. For a program containing Class 1 dates, there are two possibilities:

- Bridges are available which allow the program to be integration and system tested with other programs that have not yet been Y2K-repaired.

- If no bridges are available, the program must be held for integration testing pending availability of Y2K-fixed versions of the programs which share dependence on the same date-expanded files.

When all the tested components are available, the application is system tested to verify its correct functional operation: that it works from a business standpoint as it should. Before final release to production, most organisations carry out what is sometimes called user acceptance testing – a 'beta' test to many North Americans – by a selected group of end-users who actually *know* the application software and how to 'stretch' it. After this test, the application may be signed-off as accepted by the end-user department.

User acceptance

Defining the terms of user acceptance is one of the most difficult aspects of any specification or – particularly – contract for supply of software to a third party. If your organisation has an end-user department, subsidiary or related business for which the Y2K project team is repairing application software, treat the issue of end-user acceptance with care.

The essence of the difficulty is this: *what constitutes 100%-working application software?* If anything at all is wrong with it – or perceived to be wrong with it – user acceptance may not be granted. Failures can be as insignificant as a misplaced sub-header on a printed report, or as elusive as a perceived performance degradation. In any case, the software is not marked 'accepted'. A problem is created for higher management – and this will trickle down to you! If the user department or organisation for whom the application is being Y2K-repaired is contracted to pay for the repair, that payment may be held up, and the trouble really starts.

One of the risks of any remedial project such as Y2K, or when any new process or software product is introduced, is that it is easy for end-users to blame it in the event of any failure. Something went wrong which, they say, never failed before. The easy conclusion is that 'it must be something in the new program'.

At the planning stage of the Y2K project, the terms must be defined of user acceptance of the repaired applications. These terms must, as far as possible, close the loophole of user rejection for non-specific reasons. The user department or organisation must only be allowed to refuse Y2K-repaired software where there are specific, evident, reproducible, significant errors in its execution. 'Significant' is the part open to interpretation, of course, but it is impossible to make acceptance terms completely watertight. However, many reasons for rejection of the software can be disallowed if a few covering measures are taken:

- Make it clear in the terms defining user acceptance that preference alone – as opposed to significant error – cannot be used as a reason for rejecting Y2K-repaired applications.

- Use the general safety net which specifies that 'user acceptance of the modified software shall not unreasonably be withheld'.

Delivering good software, of course, goes a long way toward making such terms irrelevant. But 'covering your rear' in this way is, in my experience, both prudent and necessary.

6.4 Migration

After all the planning and testing have been completed, the newly Y2K-ready application is 'promoted' to production. Whether we now intend to migrate the application to client or server (in a non-mainframe environment, it may well be both), the process has two distinct stages:

- Deliver the application to the target system.
- Place it in production; make it 'live'.

The second stage is implemented as a procedure which is set out below. The delivery stage is concerned with how to get the newly ready application to the client and server in the first place.

Deployment

Placing the new application (at least, the server part of it) on a mainframe or UNIX server is easy; there is just one location to go to and it is a matter of installing the application to the required catalogs/directories, installing some run JCL or shell programs and, perhaps, setting some system or environment variables. Actually 'cutting over' into production with the new copy of the application is a more complex matter, for which a procedure is described below.

The job of deploying the Y2K-clean client side of the application to many clients is one that presents difficulties similar to those considered for operating systems in Chapter 4. Manual installation to a large number of client PCs is impractical. These are some of the difficulties associated with deployment over the organisation's network:

- How to deliver the repaired application front-end to the client without visiting each client PC.

- If the application is delivered over the network, how to make the clients all go 'live' with it at the same time. There may be 1,000 or 5,000 clients and to try and deploy to them all concurrently would probably crash the network.

- How to deploy the application to PCs very often running the Windows NT/2000 operating system, making the correct user settings and not being stopped in deploying by the operating system's own security and privilege system.

- If the application is large and the network bandwidth is limited, how to schedule a time for deployment when network use is low.

These are difficulties that would affect deployment of any new applications (not just Y2K-repaired) to a large number of PCs. They are given increased urgency, however, by the need for large-scale deployments forced by the Y2K problem. These deployments include not only repaired applications, but also tools and utilities such as inventory programs and BIOS test and fix software. Getting them to large numbers of PCs may also present a major difficulty.

On the face of it, the cleanest solution is to include repaired applications and utilities in the gold build of operating system, network software and applications referred to in Chapter 4. But co-ordinating the contents of gold builds and compiling is difficult, not something that will be done in most organisations more than once every few months. This does not allow for interim deployments of Y2K-ready applications fast coming on stream.

One solution is not to deploy the front-end of the application to PCs at all, but to allow each user to run a copy from the PCs' LAN server. This greatly reduces the scalability problem: there will be relatively few LAN servers to deploy to. The disadvantages are that a large number of PC users on each LAN become dependent on its server for continued operation of the application, and network traffic on each LAN is increased as data and programs are copied between the LAN server and each PC.

The alternative is to use a software deployment utility of the type that I refer to in Chapter 3: IBM's Tivoli; Computer Associates' UniCenter; Amdahl's Enterprise Desktop Manager; Microsoft's SMS. While powerful, these programs require a major investment in time and expertise to master. One good thing is that, in deploying application software to clients, there is at least an operating system and network software in place on the client PC; the problem is less difficult than the one of deploying system software, briefly described in Chapter 4.

The problem is nonetheless a challenging one: when fixing client applications for Y2K, your organisation will have to find a way to get the front-end modules out to the remote clients. If there are many clients, you will want to do it without visiting them all. One of the methods described above must be considered.

Going 'live'

The steps involved in 'cutting over' a centralised application are more straightforward than those of client deployment, and better understood. The process is still not simple, however, requiring as it does significant pre-planning and expertise in execution. Here is a generic list of steps that your organisation should consider when migrating from the current version of a centralised application program to the Y2K-compliant version.

Install the Year2000-ready production system environment:

- If necessary, co-ordinate with vendors for any hardware installation required and then install that hardware.
- Arrange with system programmers and administrators for installation of the Y2K-compliant application.
- Install the Y2K-compliant application on the new production system.
- Convert data used by the application to Y2K-ready form:
- Load existing data into the new application's files or databases.
- Execute data conversion programs.
- Load manually-prepared data through data entry.
- Integrate the existing and converted data.
- Test the integrated data to verify data integrity.

Perform final migration testing:

- System test the different components of the application to ensure that they work correctly together.

- As a regression test, verify that the parts of the application that have no changes still run properly as changes are made to other components.

- Verify that the application handles all its transactions correctly and remains stable for a defined period of time.

- Confirm that the system can accept input from, and provide output to, other systems with which it has interfaces.

- Obtain end-user acceptance of the new system to certify the system as acceptable for production.

Place the new application in production:

- Switch the new application to production mode by defining catalog/directory locations, system parameters and environment variables, and other settings.

- Run the new and old applications in parallel.

- Phase out the old application as the new one becomes stable.

After the Y2K application cut-over, review its operation:

- Monitor and evaluate application performance, throughput, and reliability.

- Determine what application tuning is needed.

- Track and evaluate user acceptance of the new application.

As always with these kinds of lists, the procedure given cannot be an exact 'how-to' for your organisation. The best use you can make of it is as a series of prompts: items that should be examined for relevance to your circumstances.

7 | Y2K resources

7.1 Y2K software tools

The intention of this chapter is to provide in summary form some useful information about available Y2K software tools and sources of information, as well as suggesting some tips and aspects of good practice that your organisation might benefit from in implementing its Y2K project.

The problem for a chapter such as this is the sheer volume of tools and information available, together with the fact that neither this nor any book can identify the problems and requirements of any specific enterprise. Every organisation is different and this book cannot specify, say, the software tools that are optimal for yours.

All that this section attempts, then, is to give an outline of the Y2K software utilities available from a few prominent suppliers. These suppliers are included because they are well-known and I have used some of their products. No inference should be drawn from their inclusion here. Similarly, the exclusion of hundreds of other utilities should not be construed as meaning that they are somehow not recommended. It would simply be not meaningful for a book like this to include longs lists of hundreds of suppliers and thousands of software products. There are many sites on the Web, and other sources, where you can find this kind of voluminous, detailed, information.

Note that, where Web URLs (site addresses) are given in this chapter, they are accurate at the time of writing but they may not remain so. The Web, and its site locations and addresses, are changing all the time, so be prepared to do a little searching if a site given here has been relocated or seems to have disappeared.

Following is a summary list of Y2K tool suppliers and their products.

BDM International, Inc.

Web site: www.bdm.com

Products: SMART/2000 Conversion Service, SMART Validator, SMART Manager.

Platforms: Mainframe and Client-Server.

Languages: COBOL, JCL, Natural, PL/1.

The SMART/2000 project management utility spans the lifecycle of a Y2K project, from awareness of the Y2K issues to the initial assessment of the client's inventory to actual implementation of the modified code. BDM's methodology allows the choice of either a comprehensive phased approach or selection of a single phase that can be executed independently to address the client's specific needs. BDM selects the most appropriate tools to each customer's unique requirements.

The seven phases in the SMART/2000 methodology include awareness, inventory, assessment, migration planning, renovation, testing/validation, and implementation/integration. The first three phases, awareness, inventory, and assessment, gain client understanding and acceptance of the problem, look at the client's entire business environment, and then determine the extent of the client's century date problem. The migration planning phase evaluates all possible solutions, then recommends the most appropriate solution to the client. The renovation, testing/validation and implementation/integration phases modify the source code, test the revised code, and then integrate the code into production.

BDM SMART Validator provides an enterprise-wide approach to validate renovated applications, associated software, hardware systems and interfaces, and non-information systems that are currently in production and could be date-sensitive. The program enables an organisation to evaluate and track the compliance process across multiple Y2K projects and proves that affected automated systems are millennium ready.

An extension of BDM's end-to-end SMART/2000 solution, BDM SMART Manager helps establish a program management office (PMO) to oversee enterprise-wide efforts and create a focal point for internal and external stakeholders.

Computer Associates International, Inc.

Web Site: www.cai.com

Products: CA Discovery 2000, CA-Impact/2000, CA-Endeavor, CA-Accuchek.

Platforms: Impact, MVS, VM, VSE, CICS, UNIX, Windows.

Languages: COBOL and CA-EasyTrieve, CA-ADS, PL/I, RPG.

CA Discovery 2000 is a combination of software and services incorporating automated solutions for every phase of a Y2K effort – from initial portfolio assessment through code conversion, validation and testing to final production turnover.

Many tools are provided that support aspects of year 2000 projects, including CA-Realia, CA-COBOLVISION for code management, CA-EasyTrieve for data conversion, CA -DATAMACS and CA-EZETEST for testing support.

CA-Accuchek automates the comparison of data sets and reports on the differences. It can compare entire files, specific records, or specific fields. It can compare data sets with different record formats and different record layouts. It presents output reports in a variety of formats, enabling programmers to evaluate testing results quickly. With CA-Accuchek, programmers can optionally include or exclude specific records, or ignore data that does not need to be compared.

Edge Information Group

Web Site: www.ccai.net/y2kf0250.htm

Products: Edge Portfolio Analyzer, Bridge to the Next Century.

Platforms: MVS.

Portfolio Analyzer supports initial assessment for system date impacts. Its output includes a report detailing the attributes of each MVS load module. It identifies the language product (the version of the COBOL compiler, for example) used in creation of the load module. It also enumerates the facilities used by each load module and whether the programs are CICS-based or use DB2.

Bridge to the Next Century simulates COBOL 85's date-related intrinsic functions for installations not yet using compilers that support them.

Global Software, Inc.

Web Site: www.global-software.com

Product: Giles.

Platforms: MVS, IMS.

Languages: JCL, CICS, COBOL, PL/1, Assembler, Natural, Easytrieve, Mantis, Fortran, Model 204 User Language, Model 204, ADABAS, DB2, SQL, System 2000.

Giles provides Y2K detection, inventory, and impact analysis to run on MVS using a parsing engine that can be adapted to handle additional languages, requires minimal human intervention, executes very efficiently, and provides a permanent directory of components. Giles interfaces with tools within the dictionary/repository market including automated naming tools and other data administration aids.

International Business Machines

Web Site: www.software.ibm.com/year2000/index.html

Products: TRANSFORMATION 2000 Solutions; COMUDAS; MDCT; ATC; VisualAge 2000.

Platforms: MVS, VM, VSE, AS/400, OS/2, Windows NT.

TRANSFORMATION 2000 is a comprehensive set of solutions that takes into account applications, systems software and hardware in both centralized and distributed environments. The components of TRANSFORMATION 2000 solutions are: assessment and atrategy – providing a documented strategy, cost estimates, timeframes and resources required; detailed analysis and planning – providing in-depth analysis of each of the Year-2000 affected areas of your organisation; implementation and testing – automating the changes required to source code and data; and Y2K clean management – protecting investment in application and data modifications.

The Millennium Date Compression Tool (MDCT) changes customer data while applications are running. The Application Testing Collection (ATC) offers enhanced testing capabilities for IBM's Visual Age offering reducing testing time and increasing confidence in the results for exercising Assembler, PL/I and COBOL applications on the S/390.

VisualAge 2000 is a combination with several IBM products of offerings from Edge Information Group and Isogon Corp. into a complete cross-language Y2K solution for the MVS, VM and VSE operating environments.

Isogon Corporation

Web Site: www.isogon.com/2000.htm

Products: TICTOC, SoftAudit/2000, and SoftAudit/ONE.

Platforms: IBM System/390-type mainframes under MVS/XA, MVS/ESA.

Languages: Assembler, CICS.

The SoftAudit/2000 inventory system quantifies and locates your organisation's software. It assists creation of a detailed inventory of load and source modules, and then relates that inventory to usage, giving a clear and organized view of all home-grown software.

SoftAudit/ONE gives the capability of finding the information required to ensure that your organisation is only running Y2K-compliant vendor products. It helps create a usage-based inventory of the vendor software on OS/390 based systems by locating products identifying them and monitoring their usage.

The TICTOC date simulator allows programs to be tested with 'virtual' dates later than December 31 1999, without dedicating a separate system to testing or affecting other jobs running concurrently.

MicroFocus

Web Site: www.microfocus.com/year2000/y2katmf.htm

Products: SoftFactory/2000, Revolve/2000,Workbench/2000, Process/2000. Expert Y2K Services.

Platforms: DOS, Windows 95/NT, OS/2.

Languages: Assembler, COBOL, CICS, DB2, IMS, JCL, SQL.

The SoftFactory/2000 repair tool is optimized for a 'windowing' solution and identifies only those dates which require fixing, such as dates used in some calculations and comparisons. Windowing leaves the two-digit dates in place, but adds logic to differentiate between centuries.

Revolve/2000 provides an integrated environment for addressing many of the challenges of Y2K conversion projects and supports a variety of approaches including date expansion, windowing and others. It covers a full range of Y2K project activities including application inventory analysis, Y2K assessment and estimating, complete date identification, impact analysis, and code modification.

Workbench/2000 provides a workstation-based date-change testing environment for COBOL applications. Workbench/2000 supports the development and maintenance of mainframe applications in a distributed environment that includes workstations, network servers, and mainframes. Workbench/2000 integrates the MicroFocus COBOL development and testing environment with special enhancements for Y2K projects. It incorporates editing, debugging, and communications facilities as well as graphical data tools for implementing and testing Y2K modifications.

Process/2000 is a project plan developed by MicroFocus consultants to guide clients during consulting engagements to Year 2000 compliance.

Platinum Technology, Inc.

Web Site: www.platinum.com

Products: TransCentury Office solution, TransCentury Date Simulator, Final Exam, File Ager.

Platforms: PCs: Windows 95/98; Windows NT/2000.

The TransCentury Office inventory system finds and automates the process of fixing Y2K problems in a variety of desktop applications. It also identifies problems with, and automatically updates, the PC BIOS. TransCentury Office is intranet-based to support all PC users in a distributed computing environment. Users log on to their corporate intranet, complete a questionnaire for identification and tracking purposes, then select from several options to download one or more TransCentury Office modules. Once installed on the desktop, TransCentury Office recognises each potential problem at varying degrees of risk in applications such as Microsoft Excel, Lotus 1-2-3, or QuattroPro.

The TransCentury Date Simulator provides a set of COBOL conversion routines that allow applications to be tested with system date set to later than December 31 1999.

The Final Exam suite of Y2K test tools automates the software testing lifecycle for complex client/server applications. Final Exam detects hidden errors, automate repetitive testing tasks, and enforce testing completeness – while simulating multi-user environments.

TransCentury File Age is a Y2K data ageing software product useful for testing changed applications with simulated post millennium data. With File Age, it is not necessary for the user to write database conversion programs to accommodate changing date field formats. File Age converts dates following the user's choices of more than 150 date formats supported by TransCentury.

VIASOFT

Web Site:	www.viasoft.com
Products:	OnMark 2000 for PCs, ENTERPRISE 2000 and ESW2000 constituents:

Planning Phase: Viasoft's Estimate 2000, VIA/Alliance.

Code Conversion: VIA/AutoChange, VIA/Insight, VIA/SmartEdit, Bridge 2000.

Validation/Testing: VIA/SmartTest and TCA, VIA/AutoTest, VIA/ValidDate.

Platforms:	MVS, OS/2.
Languages:	COBOL, IDMS, CICS, APS, Assembler, IMS, JCL, PL/I, SQL, Model 204, EasyTrieve, Natural, Ideal, Fortran, Assembler.

OnMark 2000 offers Y2K solutions for PC and client/server environments. OnMark VAR produces a complete inventory of hardware and software on client PCs. OnMark Assess identifies problems in spreadsheets and databases. Other stages provide hardware and software component assessment and interface repair and replacement to support overall compliance objectives. Viasoft also offers a free a BIOS test and fix module, downloadable from its website.

ESW2000 combines the Existing Systems Workbench with year 2000-specific technology. Viasoft's Estimate 2000, for conversion resource estimation, and VIA/Alliance, an application-level impact tool, determine the size and scope of their conversion effort.

VIA/AutoChange is an automated change utility, while Bridge2000 does century windowing. Information obtained from Estimate 2000 is used by VIA/AutoChange and Bridge 2000 to convert code. The

VIA/SmartTest unit testing tool, the VIA/AutoTest testing automation tool and the VIA/Validate system-date changing tool provide a testing framework for demonstrating the functional equivalency of the changed code.

The FastPath 2000 project management utility is designed to reduce the risk of a year 2000 conversion by defining the steps necessary to perform an application inventory, conversion planning, code change, testing for functional equivalency, and re-implementation and validation of the new year 2000-sensitive code. FastPath 2000 addresses the entire life cycle of a year 2000 conversion.

Cross-referenced database search

In searching for the best set of Y2K tools for the purposes of your organisation, you could try some of the many Web sites that carry out a database search for these tools. Usually, you enter a number of specifications about your organisation's line of business, computer system, application language, operating system and so on. There are no guarantees, but try theDurham Systems Management site:

www.satley.com

and see what the database search suggests for your organisation.

7.2 Sources of information

The previous section is about software tools; this one groups together a number of sources of Y2K-related information which I have found useful. Mostly, they are specific UK-based Web sites. Part of the problem inherent in looking for Y2K information is the enormous volume of material 'out there' on the Web, most of which originates in the United States. If you look for sites based in the United Kingdom, the volume of information to be waded through is drastically reduced.

Whittled down, the resulting sites prove excellent in their content and depth. The advice and information given about Year 2000 are valid in any country. If your organisation is UK-based, however, you will find that the legal advice offered is quite different from most of the US-oriented material found on the Web, and is probably more relevant to your needs.

There follow two lists of Web site addresses. The first is UK-based and grouped under the headings Government, Associations and Suppliers. The second is an international list of useful sites.

UK-based Y2K Web sites

Government

CCTA   www.ccta.gov.uk
(Central Computer and Telecommications Agency)

DTI Action 2000   www.bug2000.co.uk
(Department of Trade and Industry)

MoD   www.mod.uk
(Ministry of Defence)

SOCITM   www.socitm.gov.uk
(Society of Information Technology Management)

Taskforce 2000   www.taskforce2000.co.uk
(Confederation of British Industry (CBI) and Computer Software and Services Association (CSSA))

National Audit Office   www.open.gov.uk

Parliament   www.parliament.the-stationery-office.co.uk
(Parliament's Select Committee on Science and Technology)

Associations

IEE   www.iee.org.uk
(Institution of Electrical Engineers)

BCS   www.bcs.org.uk
(British Computer Society)

BSI   www.bsi.org.uk
(British Standards Institute)

CSSA   www.cssa.co.uk

Year 2000 Support Centre   www.support2000.com

Suppliers

Year 2000 Guide   2000.jbaworld.com
(Sponsored by IBM and JBA)

Year 2000 Millenium Resource site   www.year2000.co.uk
(Durham Systems Management)

Year 2000 Resources   www.wormhole.demon.co.uk

Interactive Training Technologies   www.itrain.co.uk

Tarlo Lyons Legal Site   www.tarlo-lyons.com

Year 2000 Law Network   www.comlinks.com/legal/lmenu.htm

International Y2K Web sites

de Jager Corporation   www.year2000.com

IBM Year 2000 Technical Support
   www.software.ibm.com/year2000

Gartner Group   www.gartner.com

SPR (Software Productivity Research) www.spr.com

Mitre Corporation   www.mitre.org/research/y2k

UK Y2K publications

British Computer Society
The Year 2000, A Practical Guide, Volume 2
ISBN 0-901865-98-2
UK£15 (members) £20 (non-members)
+44 01793 417424

National Audit Office
Managing the Millenium Threat II
Report by the Comptroller and Auditor General
ISBN 0-102962-98-7
UK£9.85

CCTA
Tackling the Year 2000 (6 volumes)
Free to members of the CCTA Year 2000 Foundation
+44 800 146020

These lists are only a tiny sample (albeit a very good sample, I think) of the Year 2000 information and resources available on the Web. The addresses given will certainly serve as a starting point for your Web exploration on the subject. Be careful, though. It is possible to waste a great deal of time 'surfing', particularly if you are not searching for a specific item.

7.3 Y2K tips

This section is a distillation of some of the more important recommendations that are presented at one place or another in this book. Some of the tips are technical and oriented toward programming techniques. Others, and probably the more important ones, are more organisational in character. I believe all of them to be crucial in implementing a Y2K project, from both the technical and business standpoints.

Business

Get management support for the Y2K project and its implementation. Without the support and commitment of the highest management, Y2K will be a project that end-users will try to ignore.

Establish a Y2K Project Office, headed by a Y2K project manager. This should be a senior manager with budgetary authority.

Ensure end-user departments take ownership of their part of the project. If Y2K is imposed on such departments, the project may still succeed, but active participation by those who will be directly affected improves the chances of this.

The Y2K project office should mount a campaign of awareness within the organisation, encouraging departments to take ownership of their part of the problem.

The Y2K project manager must have a sufficient budget and the authority to spend it. If responsibility for implementing Y2K is not matched by authority to spend money to achieve it, the project will fail.

Make realistic cost estimates. Using a lines-of-code cost approximate will result in an underestimate for the project as a whole. The budget should include provisions for all parts of the system — clients and servers included — and for testing.

The Y2K project manager must have the right to approve and, if necessary, veto, all other software development and procurement within the organisation in the run up to 2000.

Check the credentials of Y2K consultants. In particular identify their previous Y2K project experience and get references from their employers on these projects.

Retain a legal adviser, if only for occasional use during the Y2K project's lifetime.

Take great care in devising post-Y2K-test end-user acceptance criteria. It is easy for the end-user to blame a perceived or real malfunction on the Y2K project when in fact Y2K is not the culprit. In signing-off acceptance of Y2K-fixed applications, the user must be discouraged from unreasonably withholding acceptance.

Systems management

Back up all valuable data files before performing Y2K fixes on any system. In practice, this means system administration staff taking copies of server data files, with individual users being responsible for backing up PC data.

The client is a greater problem than the server. I have repeated this throughout the book. Wherever scalability is an issue (lots of PCs compared to a few servers), the Y2K problem multiplies. Many publications give insufficient attention to PCs because it is a difficult aspect of the problem and because the process of fixing server software is better understood. Look to your PCs.

Fixing the client consists of much more than a CMOS/BIOS check. The client operating system and applications may have to be upgraded as part of the Y2K fix; these upgrades are far more complex than fixing the PC system clock.

Replace a PC in preference to upgrading or reprogramming its BIOS. Upgraded PC hardware often fails to work or later causes other problems of compatibility.

Initialise client PCs from a standard gold build, not on an ad-hoc basis. If your organisation has even 50, never mind 500, PCs that were individually manually installed, the problem of subsequently supporting them becomes difficult, if not intractable.

Upgrade client PCs to one standard configuration. Many organisations, in attempting to support their stock of PCs, are plagued by the fact of having many different, possibly incompatible configurations. Using the Y2K-fix necessity as an opportunity to homogenise the organisation's PCs makes subsequent support of them much easier.

Use the Y2K fix necessity as an opportunity to streamline the organisation's software base and to implement PC and operating system upgrades.

Take the LAN server off-line when unit-testing client PCs for Y2K readiness. Even though the PCs BIOS and clock may be correct, its setting may be overridden by the server.

In networks extending over multiple time zones, test the cases where clients are recording different dates than are network and application servers.

Performance is not an issue. Extra code and processing is caused by the Y2K repair. It may prompt acquisition of extra, larger, more-powerful equipment. But the impact in terms of execution speed is very slight and can be ignored.

For shrink-wrapped client applications, check on the Web or with the supplier availability of free fixes before paying to upgrade the applications.

Programming

Do not define 'mission critical' too tightly. Production of invoices is mission critical. Printing them in sorted order may be deemed not mission critical, but it is very inconvenient when thousands of unsorted invoices are produced.

Make only necessary changes. Classify dates that appear in programs and files. Only Class 1 dates require date expansion and associated code change. Class 2 dates only require windowing. Class 3 dates need no work at all. The saving in applying this method compared with the change-everything approach is at least a factor of 5.

Append expanded dates to file records; do not change dates in place. This greatly reduces the effort in writing bridge programs, and their complexity.

Bridges should be one-way: they should be used to 'strip down' date-expanded files to their original form so that old applications can use the data. To remove the possibility of file corruption, bridges must not be used to update Y2K-compliant data-expanded files.

Search specially for literals. Code containing numeric literals used (or not) in date operations can be hard to identify. '00' and '99' particularly can have end-of-file or other special meanings. And who is to say that '75' is or is not a date?

Co-ordinate required data formats with suppliers and customers. Any two organisations that share data containing date-dependencies must agree rules for processing that data. These rules will be expressed as terms of compliance required by either side.

Testing

Collect all client Y2K fixes together on a gold build. Test the build in a central test 'shop', avoiding the need to conduct testing on every individual client PC.

Test the gold build with important boundary dates (see page 127).

Test only what must be tested. There are two main ways of restricting the scope of the test effort: reduction of client testing to checking CMOS and BIOS; and using date classification on the server to minimise application testing. The first may be possible if operating system and PC application software upgrades are unnecessary. The second should always be applied. Reducing the scope of the Y2K test effort is central to keeping the project schedule on track.

Eliminate the need to test server applications, where possible. Applications containing only Class 3 dates and to which no non-Y2K change has been made need not be tested as part of the Y2K project.

Test server applications stand-alone where possible. Stand-alone testing is all that is necessary for applications containing only Class 2 and 3 dates and, therefore, all that should be done.

Use bridges to allow stand-alone testing of applications containing Class 1 dates.

Carry out server application testing on a dedicated, off-line, testing system. Mixing test and production systems on the same physical computer system is a bad idea.

In testing server applications, keep test cases and data minimised, specific and targeted. One targeted test case may exercise a given function as well as 1,000 test cases. Large amounts of test data produce voluminous test output, analysis of which requires more time to be scheduled as part of the test effort.

Small Business

Many small business will not encounter the server part of the Y2K problem — they may have no server to worry about. Their difficulty may be restricted to date dependencies found on PCs and, perhaps, a network server. The scope of the problem is accordingly reduced to that of the client component. If client PCs have Y2K-compliant BIOSs and only shrink-wrapped software is used, there may be no Y2K problem at all. Simple testing of the BIOS and applications will verify whether or not this is the case.

Small businesses heavily dependent on large client organisations should take care to comply with these organisations' Y2K requirements and to document that compliance. If necessary, legal advice should be taken here.

In evaluating the scale of their Y2K problem — if they have one — small business should briefly hire a Y2K consultant to set the direction of the Y2K project, however limited it may be.

Conclusion

This book attempts to address all aspects of the Year 2000 problem as it affects an organisation's computer hardware and software. Large enterprises — banks, oil companies and so on — may have a 'handle' on the problem, even if they have not yet fixed it. There are many more small businesses which have not even started the process of Y2K evaluation. They should not panic. They may have no Y2K problem at all and, even if they have, it will be of more limited character that that of the banks and oil companies. What they must not do is either ignore the problem or succumb to the hype which blows it out of proportion. Sober analysis of their situation using, I hope, some of the suggestions in this book as prompts, should enable them to come through the Great Day unscathed.

Index